The Ultimate Guide to Animal Behavior

Understanding Your Pets and Wildlife in Their
Natural Habitats

Lonnie Webb

The Ultimate Guide to Animal Behavior

TABLE OF CONTENTS

Chapter 1: Understanding Your Pets

Common Pet Behaviors and Their Meanings

Understanding the behaviors of our pets is crucial to forging a stronger bond and ensuring their well-being. Pets, particularly dogs and cats, exhibit a wide range of behaviors that can be both endearing and perplexing. Decoding these behaviors can help pet owners respond appropriately and create a more harmonious living environment.

Dogs, as descendants of wolves, have retained many instinctual behaviors that served their ancestors well. One of the most common behaviors is the wagging tail. While a wagging tail often indicates happiness, the context and manner of the wag can alter its meaning. A broad, sweeping wag usually signifies a friendly greeting, while a stiff, rapid wag can indicate anxiety or agitation. Similarly, a tucked tail often signals fear or submission, suggesting that the dog feels threatened or uncomfortable.

Barking is another behavior that can vary widely in meaning. It can serve as a greeting, a warning, or an expression of excitement. Understanding the pitch, duration, and frequency of the bark can provide clues to the dog's emotional state. High-pitched, intermittent barks often signal excitement or playfulness, whereas low, continuous barking can indicate a perceived threat or an attempt to protect territory.

Cats, on the other hand, communicate more subtly. Their body language and vocalizations can be nuanced and require keen observation. Purring is commonly associated with contentment, but cats may also purr when they are in pain or distressed as a self-soothing mechanism. The context in which the purring occurs is key to understanding its true meaning.

Tail movements in cats can also be quite telling. A tail held high usually indicates a confident, happy cat, while a puffed-up tail signifies fear or aggression. A twitching tail can be a sign of irritation or excitement. Additionally, the positioning of a cat's ears can provide insight into their mood. Forward-facing ears typically indicate curiosity or interest, whereas flattened ears suggest fear or aggression.

Understanding the meaning behind pet behaviors is not only about interpreting body language but also recognizing patterns and changes. For example, a dog that suddenly begins to chew furniture or dig excessively may be experiencing anxiety or boredom. Providing mental stimulation through toys, training, and regular exercise can alleviate these behaviors. Similarly, a cat that starts to urinate outside the litter box might be signaling a medical issue or stress. Consulting a veterinarian can help identify underlying health problems or environmental stressors.

Pets also express their needs and emotions through vocalizations. Dogs may whine to communicate discomfort, anxiety, or a desire for attention. It's important to address the underlying cause of the whining rather than simply trying to stop the behavior. Cats, known for their more reserved nature, can be quite vocal when they want to be. Meowing can serve various purposes, from greeting their owners to demanding food or expressing discomfort. Each cat has its unique set of vocalizations, and attentive owners can learn to distinguish between them.

Social behaviors are another important aspect of understanding pets. Dogs are pack animals and thrive on social interaction. They may exhibit behaviors like jumping, licking, or leaning against their owners to seek attention and affection. Training can help manage these behaviors, teaching dogs more appropriate ways to interact. Socialization with other dogs and people from a young age is crucial for developing well-rounded, confident pets.

Cats are generally more solitary but still require social interaction, especially with their human companions. They may head-butt, knead, or follow their owners around as expressions of affection. While cats often enjoy their independence, they also benefit from play and engagement with their owners. Interactive toys and scheduled playtime can help satisfy their need for stimulation and prevent behavioral issues born out of boredom or frustration.

Behavioral problems in pets can stem from various sources, including genetics, environment, and past experiences. It's important to approach these issues with patience and understanding. For instance, a dog that exhibits aggression may have had negative experiences or lack of socialization. Working with a professional trainer or behaviorist can help address these issues through positive reinforcement techniques.

Cats, too, can develop behavioral problems such as scratching furniture or excessive grooming. Providing appropriate outlets for these behaviors, like scratching posts and regular grooming sessions, can mitigate their impact. Environmental enrichment, such as climbing structures and puzzle feeders, can also help keep cats mentally and physically stimulated.

One of the most rewarding aspects of understanding pet behavior is enhancing the bond between pet and owner. Recognizing and responding to the needs and emotions of pets fosters trust and deepens the relationship. Simple actions like making eye contact, speaking in a calm and soothing voice, and spending quality time together can significantly strengthen this bond.

Pets also benefit from routines and consistency. Regular feeding times, exercise schedules, and training sessions provide structure and predictability, which can reduce anxiety and promote well-being. Consistent responses to behaviors, whether through rewards or gentle corrections, help pets understand expectations and feel secure.

In some cases, professional help may be necessary to address complex behavioral issues. Veterinary behaviorists and certified animal behaviorists can provide valuable insights and tailored intervention strategies. They can help identify underlying medical conditions, recommend behavior modification techniques, and guide owners through the process of addressing challenging behaviors.

Ultimately, understanding common pet behaviors and their meanings is a journey of discovery and empathy. It requires observing, listening, and responding to pets in ways that honor their unique personalities and needs. By doing so, pet owners can create a nurturing environment that promotes happiness, health, and harmony for both pets and their human companions.

Training Techniques for Dogs and Cats

Training pets is both an art and a science, requiring patience, consistency, and a deep understanding of animal behavior. Whether you're training a dog or a cat, the principles remain the same: positive reinforcement, clear communication, and gradual progression. Let's explore some effective techniques to help you successfully train your furry companions.

Dogs are social animals that thrive on structure and guidance. One of the most fundamental aspects of training is establishing yourself as the leader in a way that is both firm and compassionate. Dogs look to their owners for cues and direction, so consistency in commands and expectations is key. Start with basic commands like "sit," "stay," and "come." These commands form the foundation for more complex behaviors and help create a language between you and your dog.

Positive reinforcement is the cornerstone of effective dog training. This method involves rewarding desired behaviors with treats, praise, or play. For instance, when teaching a dog to sit, hold a treat close to its nose and slowly move it upward, causing the dog to naturally sit. As soon as the dog sits, reward it with the treat and verbal praise. Repeating this process reinforces the behavior, making the dog more likely to sit on command in the future.

Consistency is crucial. Use the same command word and reward every time. Dogs learn through repetition, and varying the command or reward can confuse them. Additionally, keep training sessions short—about 10 to 15 minutes—to maintain the dog's attention and enthusiasm. Regular, brief sessions are more effective than occasional, longer ones.

One common challenge in dog training is housebreaking. Consistency and patience are essential here as well. Establish a regular feeding schedule and take your dog outside to the same spot shortly after eating. Praise and reward the dog immediately after it eliminates outside. If accidents occur indoors, clean them thoroughly to remove any scent that might attract the dog back to the same spot. Never punish the dog for accidents, as this can create fear and anxiety, complicating the training process.

Leash training is another important aspect. Start by letting your dog get used to wearing a collar and leash indoors. Once comfortable, practice walking in a distraction-free environment. Keep the leash short but loose, and use treats to encourage the dog to walk beside you. If the dog pulls, stop walking and stand still until the leash relaxes, then resume walking. This teaches the dog that pulling doesn't get it where it wants to go.

Cats, while often perceived as independent and aloof, can also be trained using similar principles. The key to training cats is understanding their unique motivations and working with their natural behaviors. Unlike dogs, cats are not pack animals and may not respond to commands in the same way. However, they are highly intelligent and can learn a variety of behaviors with the right approach.

Litter box training is usually straightforward with cats, as they have a natural instinct to bury their waste. Provide a clean, accessible litter box and place the cat in it shortly after meals or naps. Most cats will quickly understand its purpose. If issues arise, consider the location of the litter box, the type of litter, and cleanliness. Cats are particular about their environment and may refuse to use a box that doesn't meet their standards.

Teaching a cat to come when called can be very useful, especially for indoor-outdoor cats. Use a distinct sound, such as a clicker or a specific call, and pair it with a high-value treat. Call the cat's name and make the sound, then immediately reward the cat when it responds. Over time, the cat will associate the sound with positive outcomes and will be more likely to come when called.

Scratching is a natural behavior for cats, but it can be problematic when directed at furniture. Provide appropriate outlets like scratching posts or pads. Encourage your cat to use these by placing them in areas where the cat likes to scratch and rewarding the cat for using them. If the cat scratches furniture, gently redirect it to the scratching post and reward it for scratching there. Using deterrents like double-sided tape on furniture can also discourage unwanted scratching.

Clicker training, often associated with dogs, can be highly effective for cats as well. The clicker is a tool that makes a distinct sound, used to mark desired behaviors at the precise moment they occur. For example, if you're teaching a cat to sit, wait for the cat to naturally sit, click the moment it does, and then reward it. The click signals to the cat that it did something right, and the reward reinforces the behavior.

Training sessions with cats should be even shorter than with dogs, generally around 5 to 10 minutes. Cats can become easily bored or overstimulated, so keeping sessions brief and ending on a positive note is important. Patience is key, as cats may take longer to respond to training than dogs.

Both dogs and cats benefit from socialization, which is an integral part of training. Exposing them to different people, environments, and experiences in a controlled manner helps them become well-adjusted and reduces fear and anxiety. For dogs, this might include visits to the park, meeting other dogs, or having friends over. For cats, it could involve gentle handling by different people, exploring different rooms, and experiencing various sounds and smells.

Addressing behavioral issues often requires understanding the underlying cause. For instance, a dog that barks excessively might be bored, anxious, or seeking attention. Identifying and addressing the root cause—through increased exercise, mental stimulation, or training—can reduce the unwanted behavior. Similarly, a cat that urinates outside the litter box might be experiencing stress, a medical issue, or dissatisfaction with the litter box. Consulting a veterinarian or professional trainer can provide additional insights and strategies.

Training pets is a rewarding journey that strengthens the bond between owner and animal. It requires time, patience, and a commitment to understanding the unique needs and behaviors of your pet. By using positive reinforcement, maintaining consistency, and approaching training with empathy, you can teach your pets to be well-behaved and happy members of your household.

Socialization: The Key to Happy Pets

Socialization is a critical aspect of raising well-adjusted pets, playing a pivotal role in their behavioral development and overall happiness. Proper socialization helps animals become confident, reduces anxiety, and prevents behavioral issues. By exposing pets to a variety of experiences, people, and environments during their formative periods, owners can ensure their pets grow into well-rounded companions.

For dogs, the socialization window is typically between 3 and 14 weeks of age. This period is crucial because puppies are naturally curious and more receptive to new experiences. During this time, exposing them to different environments, sounds, sights, and people can significantly impact their future behavior. Begin by introducing your puppy to various household items like vacuum cleaners, televisions, and different types of flooring. Gradually move on to outdoor experiences such as walks in the park, car rides, and visits to pet-friendly stores.

One effective technique is to organize playdates with other vaccinated puppies and friendly adult dogs. These interactions teach puppies essential social skills, including bite inhibition, appropriate play behavior, and the ability to read other dogs' body language. Supervise these encounters to ensure positive interactions and intervene if play becomes too rough. Remember, the goal is to create positive associations, so reward your puppy with treats and praise for calm and friendly behavior.

Exposure to different types of people is equally important. Introduce your puppy to individuals of varying ages, sizes, and appearances. Encourage gentle interactions and use treats to reinforce positive behavior. It's beneficial to include people wearing hats, sunglasses, or uniforms, as these can sometimes be intimidating to dogs. Regular, positive experiences with diverse groups of people help prevent fear and aggression later in life.

Sounds can be a common source of anxiety for dogs. Gradually acclimate your puppy to different noises such as thunderstorms, fireworks, and household appliances. Start with low volumes and gradually increase the intensity, always rewarding calm behavior. There are also sound desensitization programs and recordings available that can aid in this process.

For cats, socialization is most effective when started between 2 and 7 weeks of age. However, older cats can still benefit from gradual exposure to new experiences. Begin by creating a safe, quiet space for your kitten or cat to retreat to if they feel overwhelmed. Slowly introduce new stimuli, ensuring each experience is positive and stress-free.

Handling is a critical component of socializing cats. Gently handle your kitten frequently, including touching their paws, ears, and mouth. This not only helps them become accustomed to human touch but also makes future grooming and veterinary visits less stressful. Offer treats and gentle praise to reinforce their comfort with handling.

Introducing cats to other animals requires patience and careful planning. When introducing a new kitten to a household with other pets, start by allowing them to sniff each other through a closed door. Gradually progress to supervised face-to-face meetings, using treats to create positive associations. Monitor their interactions closely and separate them if any signs of aggression or fear arise. Over time, with patience and positive reinforcement, most cats can learn to coexist peacefully with other animals.

Enriching your cat's environment is another important aspect of socialization. Provide a variety of toys, scratching posts, and climbing structures to keep them mentally and physically stimulated. Regular play sessions with interactive toys help strengthen the bond between you and your cat while also providing essential exercise.

Socialization doesn't end after the initial critical period. Continued exposure to new experiences throughout a pet's life is essential for maintaining their social skills. Regularly introduce your pet to new environments, people, and animals to keep their socialization skills sharp. For dogs, enrolling in training classes or participating in dog sports can provide ongoing opportunities for social interaction and mental stimulation.

Traveling with your pets, whether it's a trip to the vet or a vacation, can be a significant aspect of their socialization. For dogs, start by taking short car rides to acclimate them to the experience. Use a secure crate or harness and gradually increase the length of the trips, always ending with a positive experience such as a walk or a treat. For cats, ensure their carrier is comfortable and familiar by leaving it out in the home and placing treats or toys inside. Short trips around the block can help them become accustomed to car travel.

Preventing and addressing fear and aggression is a crucial part of socialization. If your pet exhibits fear or aggressive behavior, it's important to address it promptly. For dogs, counter-conditioning and desensitization techniques can be very effective. This involves gradually exposing the dog to the source of fear at a low intensity and pairing it with something positive, like treats or play. Over time, the dog's response to the fear-inducing stimulus should improve.

For cats, creating a safe and calm environment is essential. If a cat is fearful or aggressive, provide high perches or hiding spots where they can retreat and feel secure. Gradually expose them to the source of their fear in a controlled manner, using treats and praise to create positive associations. In both cases, consulting with a professional trainer or behaviorist can provide additional strategies and support.

Socialization also includes teaching pets to be comfortable with routine care activities. For dogs, this might involve regular grooming, nail trims, and dental care. Start by handling your dog's paws, ears, and mouth gently, rewarding them for staying calm. Gradually progress to using grooming tools, always pairing the experience with positive reinforcement. For cats, regular brushing and nail trims should be introduced gradually, using treats and praise to make the experience pleasant.

It's essential to recognize that every pet is unique and may require different approaches to socialization. Some pets may be naturally more confident and outgoing, while others may be shy or fearful. Tailor your socialization efforts to your pet's individual needs and progress at a pace they're comfortable with. Patience and persistence are key to successful socialization.

The benefits of proper socialization are far-reaching. Well-socialized pets are typically more confident, less stressed, and better behaved. They are also less likely to develop behavioral problems such as aggression, excessive barking, or destructive behavior. Moreover, socialized pets are easier to handle during grooming, veterinary visits, and other routine care activities, making life more enjoyable for both the pet and the owner.

Socialization is a lifelong process that requires ongoing effort and attention. By providing your pets with positive experiences and exposing them to a variety of stimuli, you can help them become well-adjusted, happy, and confident members of your family. Remember, the goal is to create a positive association with new experiences, ensuring that your pets feel safe and secure in their environment. With patience, consistency, and a lot of love, you can unlock the full potential of your furry companions and enjoy a harmonious and fulfilling relationship with them.

Addressing Behavioral Problems

Behavioral problems in pets can be a major source of stress for both the animals and their owners. Understanding the root causes and implementing effective strategies to address these issues is crucial for fostering a harmonious living environment. This chapter delves into practical methods for identifying, managing, and preventing common behavioral problems in pets.

Understanding the underlying causes of behavioral issues is the first step in addressing them. Often, these problems stem from unmet needs, such as lack of exercise, inadequate socialization, or inconsistent training. For instance, a dog that barks excessively may be seeking attention, feeling anxious when left alone, or simply bored. Similarly, a cat that urinates outside the litter box might be experiencing stress, a medical issue, or dissatisfaction with the litter box setup.

Observation is key to identifying the triggers for your pet's behavior. Take note of the circumstances in which the problem occurs, including the time of day, the presence of certain people or animals, and any environmental changes. Keeping a behavior journal can be immensely helpful in spotting patterns and pinpointing specific triggers. Once you have a clear understanding of the causes, you can begin to address them effectively.

Consistency in training and routine is essential for managing behavioral problems. Pets thrive on predictability, and a structured environment helps them feel secure. Establish a daily routine that includes regular feeding times, exercise, and training sessions. Consistent rules and boundaries should be enforced by all family members to avoid confusion and reinforce desired behaviors.

Positive reinforcement is one of the most effective methods for modifying behavior. This involves rewarding your pet for displaying good behavior, which encourages them to repeat it. Rewards can include treats, praise, or playtime. For example, if your dog jumps on guests, reward them for sitting calmly instead. Consistency is crucial; ensure that rewards are given immediately after the desired behavior occurs to reinforce the connection.

Addressing specific behavioral problems requires targeted strategies. For dogs with separation anxiety, creating a safe and comfortable space where they can relax when left alone is important. Gradually increase the time you spend away from home, starting with short periods and slowly extending them. Leaving a piece of clothing with your scent can provide comfort, and interactive toys can help keep them occupied.

Aggression in dogs can be particularly challenging. Identifying the type of aggression—whether it's fear-based, territorial, or related to resource guarding—is crucial for determining the appropriate approach. For fear-based aggression, desensitization and counter-conditioning techniques can be effective. This involves gradually exposing the dog to the source of fear in a controlled manner while providing positive reinforcement. Professional guidance from a certified dog trainer or behaviorist is often necessary for managing aggressive behavior.

Cats can also exhibit a range of behavioral issues, such as scratching furniture, aggression toward other pets, or litter box problems. Providing appropriate outlets for natural behaviors is essential. For scratching, ensure that your cat has access to scratching posts or pads. Encourage their use by placing them in strategic locations and using catnip as an attractant. Covering furniture with double-sided tape or aluminum foil temporarily can deter scratching until the cat becomes accustomed to using the scratchers.

Inter-cat aggression often arises from territorial disputes or lack of resources. Ensure each cat has its own food and water bowls, litter box, and resting areas. Gradual introductions and supervised interactions can help reduce tension. In multi-cat households, providing vertical spaces like cat trees or shelves can help increase territory and reduce conflict.

Litter box issues can be particularly frustrating. Start by ensuring the litter box is clean and placed in a quiet, accessible location. Some cats are particular about the type of litter used, so experimenting with different options may be necessary. If the problem persists, consult a veterinarian to rule out any underlying medical issues.

Environmental enrichment plays a significant role in preventing and addressing behavioral problems. Boredom and lack of mental stimulation can lead to destructive behaviors in both dogs and cats. Providing toys, puzzle feeders, and interactive play sessions can help keep your pet mentally engaged. For dogs, regular walks, playtime, and training sessions are essential. Cats benefit from toys that mimic prey, such as feather wands and laser pointers, as well as opportunities to climb and explore.

Training classes and professional help can be invaluable resources. Enrolling in obedience classes not only provides structured training but also socialization opportunities for dogs. Professional trainers can offer personalized guidance and support, especially for more complex behavioral issues. For cats, behaviorists can provide insights into feline-specific problems and recommend tailored solutions.

Preventing behavioral problems from arising in the first place is always preferable. Early socialization and training are key components of this preventative approach. For puppies and kittens, exposing them to a variety of experiences, people, and environments during their critical developmental periods helps them grow into well-adjusted adults. Ongoing training and socialization throughout their lives ensure they remain adaptable and well-behaved.

Health and wellness also play a crucial role in behavior. Regular veterinary check-ups can help identify any medical issues that might be contributing to behavioral problems. Pain, discomfort, or illness can manifest as changes in behavior, so it's important to rule out any underlying health concerns. Providing a balanced diet, regular exercise, and mental stimulation are all integral to maintaining your pet's overall well-being.

Patience and perseverance are essential when addressing behavioral problems. Change often takes time, and setbacks are normal. It's important to stay committed to the training and behavior modification plan, even when progress seems slow. Celebrate small victories and remember that each step forward is a move toward a happier, better-behaved pet.

Addressing behavioral problems in pets requires a multifaceted approach that includes understanding the underlying causes, consistent training, positive reinforcement, and environmental enrichment. By observing your pet's behavior, identifying triggers, and implementing targeted strategies, you can effectively manage and prevent many common issues. Enlisting the help of professionals when needed and focusing on prevention through early socialization and training are also key components of a successful behavior management plan. With patience, consistency, and a comprehensive approach, you can help your pet overcome behavioral challenges and enjoy a harmonious, happy life together.

Enhancing Bonding with Your Pets

Creating and nurturing a deep bond with your pet is a rewarding journey that enriches both your life and theirs. Pets, whether dogs, cats, or other animals, thrive on companionship, trust, and love. Building a strong connection involves understanding their needs, communicating effectively, and spending quality time together. This chapter offers practical advice on enhancing the bond with your pet, ensuring a lasting and fulfilling relationship.

Understanding your pet's individual personality and preferences is crucial for bonding. Just like humans, each pet has its own unique character traits and behaviors. Spend time observing your pet to learn what they enjoy and what makes them uncomfortable. For instance, some dogs might love vigorous play sessions, while others prefer gentle walks. Cats might enjoy interactive toys or quiet lap time. Recognizing and respecting these preferences is the first step in building trust and affection.

Communication is the foundation of any strong relationship, and this holds true for pets as well. Pets rely heavily on body language, vocalizations, and even scent to communicate. Learning to read your pet's signals can prevent misunderstandings and foster a deeper connection. For example, a wagging tail generally indicates a happy dog, while a tucked tail might suggest fear or anxiety. Similarly, a cat's purring usually signals contentment, but it can also indicate discomfort if accompanied by other signs of distress. Responding appropriately to these cues—comforting them when they're scared or engaging them when they're playful—reinforces their trust in you.

Quality time is another essential component of bonding. Regularly engaging in activities that your pet enjoys strengthens your relationship and provides mental and physical stimulation. For dogs, this might include daily walks, playtime in the park, or training sessions. Training not only teaches your dog new skills but also enhances communication and understanding between you. Positive reinforcement techniques, like rewarding good behavior with treats or praise, make training a fun and bonding experience.

Cats, on the other hand, often appreciate interactive play that taps into their hunting instincts. Toys that mimic the movement of prey, such as feather wands or laser pointers, can provide hours of entertainment and exercise. Setting aside time each day for interactive play shows your cat that you value their company and enjoy spending time with them. Additionally, offering them cozy spots to relax near you, like a cat bed or a perch by the window, allows them to be close while feeling secure in their territory.

Routine and consistency are vital in strengthening the bond with your pet. Animals feel more secure when they know what to expect, so establishing a daily routine can help reduce anxiety and build trust. Regular feeding times, consistent training sessions, and predictable playtimes create a stable environment where your pet feels safe. This consistency also extends to rules and boundaries. Ensuring that all family members enforce the same rules prevents confusion and helps your pet understand what is expected of them.

Physical touch is a powerful tool for bonding with your pet. Many pets, especially dogs and cats, enjoy being petted and groomed. Regular grooming sessions not only keep your pet clean and healthy but also provide an opportunity for close physical contact. Brushing your dog's coat or gently stroking your cat's fur can be soothing for both of you. Pay attention to your pet's reactions and adjust your touch accordingly. Some pets might prefer gentle strokes, while others enjoy a more vigorous rub.

Creating positive associations is another effective way to enhance bonding. Associate your presence with good things by offering treats, toys, or affection. For example, if your dog is hesitant around new people, encourage positive interactions by rewarding them when they remain calm. Similarly, if your cat is shy, let them approach you on their terms and reward them with treats or gentle petting. Over time, your pet will start to associate you with positive experiences, strengthening your bond.

Shared experiences also play a significant role in bonding. Taking your dog on new adventures, such as hiking trails or visiting pet-friendly cafes, can create lasting memories and deepen your connection. For cats, creating a stimulating environment at home with climbing trees, scratching posts, and puzzle feeders can provide enriching experiences. Observing and participating in these activities together fosters a sense of companionship and mutual enjoyment.

Understanding and respecting your pet's boundaries is essential for a healthy relationship. Not all pets enjoy being hugged or picked up, and forcing physical affection can lead to stress and fear. Instead, let your pet initiate contact and respect their comfort levels. If your pet seems anxious or uncomfortable, give them space and time to approach you when they're ready. Building trust takes time, and respecting their boundaries is a crucial part of the process.

Bonding with your pet can also be enhanced through training and learning new skills together. Training sessions provide mental stimulation and help improve communication. Teaching your dog basic commands, tricks, or even agility exercises can be a fun and rewarding experience for both of you. Cats can also benefit from training, learning commands like "sit" or "high five" with the help of clicker training and treats. The key is to keep sessions short, positive, and consistent.

Health and well-being are fundamental to a strong bond. Regular veterinary check-ups ensure that your pet is healthy and can help identify any potential issues early. A healthy pet is typically happier and more active, making it easier to engage in bonding activities. Additionally, providing a balanced diet, regular exercise, and mental stimulation contributes to their overall well-being and strengthens your relationship.

Finally, patience and empathy are essential in building a deep bond with your pet. Every pet has its own pace of learning and adapting, and it's important to be patient and understanding throughout the process. Celebrate small victories and progress, and don't get discouraged by setbacks. Empathizing with your pet's experiences and emotions helps you connect on a deeper level and fosters a more harmonious relationship.

Enhancing bonding with your pet involves a blend of understanding, communication, shared experiences, and mutual respect. By observing their behavior, engaging in activities they enjoy, and maintaining a consistent routine, you can build a strong, trust-based relationship. Physical touch, positive associations, and respecting boundaries further deepen this connection, while training and health care contribute to their overall well-being. With patience, empathy, and a commitment to spending quality time together, you can create a lasting and fulfilling bond with your pet.

Chapter 2: Wildlife Behavior in Natural Habitats

The Role of Instinct in Animal Behavior

Instinct plays a pivotal role in shaping animal behavior, guiding their actions and reactions in ways that ensure survival and reproduction. Understanding instinctual behaviors is crucial for anyone who works with or cares for animals. These behaviors are hardwired into an animal's genetic makeup and are typically performed without prior experience or learning. They encompass a wide range of activities, from basic survival mechanisms to complex social interactions. This chapter delves into the importance of instinct in animal behavior, providing insights into how these innate actions influence the lives of pets and their interactions with their environment and humans.

One of the most fundamental instinctual behaviors observed in animals is the drive for survival. This includes finding food, avoiding predators, and seeking shelter. For instance, a cat's instinct to hunt is deeply ingrained, even in domesticated environments where food is readily provided. This hunting behavior is not necessarily about hunger but about fulfilling an intrinsic need to stalk and capture prey. Understanding this can help pet owners provide appropriate outlets for their cat's natural hunting instincts, such as interactive toys that mimic the movement of prey.

Similarly, dogs exhibit a range of survival-driven behaviors rooted in their wild ancestors. The instinct to dig, for example, can be traced back to wolves that buried food to keep it safe from scavengers. While this behavior might be inconvenient in a manicured garden, it's important to recognize its instinctual origins. Providing a designated digging area or engaging in activities that fulfill this need can help manage such behaviors in a way that's harmonious with the household environment.

Instinct also governs social behaviors, particularly in animals that live in groups or packs. Dogs, for instance, have a strong pack mentality, which influences their interactions with both humans and other animals. This pack instinct drives behaviors such as establishing dominance, showing submission, and forming hierarchies. Recognizing these social instincts can aid in training and managing dogs, ensuring they understand their place within the family "pack." Consistent training and clear boundaries help reinforce their role, reducing anxiety and promoting a stable and happy pet.

Maternal instincts are another critical aspect of animal behavior. These instincts ensure the survival of offspring through nurturing, protection, and teaching. A mother dog or cat will instinctively care for her young, guiding them through the early stages of life with behaviors that are innate rather than learned. Understanding these maternal behaviors can be particularly important for breeders or anyone caring for a pregnant or nursing pet. Providing a safe, quiet space for a mother and her young, and minimizing stressors, supports these natural instincts and promotes the well-being of both the mother and her offspring.

Migration and territorial instincts are also significant in the animal kingdom. Birds, for example, migrate vast distances guided by instinctual cues. While this behavior is less directly relevant to pet owners, understanding territorial instincts is crucial, especially for animals like cats and dogs. Cats are known for their strong territorial nature, often marking their space with scent glands located on their face and paws. This behavior helps them feel secure in their environment. For dog owners, recognizing territorial instincts can help in managing behaviors related to guarding property or reacting to perceived intruders.

Play behavior is another fascinating aspect of animal instinct. Play is not just a frivolous activity but serves important functions in development and socialization. Young animals, such as puppies and kittens, engage in play that mimics hunting, fighting, and other adult behaviors. This play helps them develop physical coordination, social skills, and problem-solving abilities. Encouraging play and providing suitable toys and environments can support these instinctual behaviors, promoting healthy development and well-being.

Instincts also play a role in communication among animals. Many species have evolved specific vocalizations, body language, and other signals to convey information. Dogs, for instance, use a combination of barking, growling, and body postures to communicate. Understanding these instinctual communication methods can enhance the bond between pets and their owners. For example, recognizing the difference between a playful bark and an alarm bark helps owners respond appropriately to their dog's needs and signals.

Fear and aggression are instinctual responses that serve to protect animals from threats. While these behaviors are essential for survival in the wild, they can sometimes manifest in undesirable ways in domesticated animals. A dog might instinctively react aggressively to a perceived threat, even if it poses no real danger. Understanding the roots of these behaviors can help in developing strategies to manage and mitigate them. For instance, socialization and gradual exposure to new experiences can help a fearful dog build confidence and reduce instinctual aggression.

Reproductive instincts drive behaviors related to mating and procreation. These instincts are powerful and can sometimes lead to challenges for pet owners, such as marking territory, mounting, or seeking out mates. Spaying or neutering pets can help manage some of these instinctual behaviors, contributing to a more harmonious household. Additionally, providing mental and physical stimulation can help channel these energies into more acceptable activities.

Understanding the role of instinct in animal behavior also involves recognizing the limitations and boundaries of training and behavior modification. While training can shape and influence behavior, it's essential to respect the instinctual drives that are deeply embedded in an animal's nature. For example, training a herding dog to suppress its instinct to chase can be challenging, but providing appropriate outlets for this behavior, such as agility training or herding activities, can satisfy these instincts in a controlled manner.

Instinctual behaviors can sometimes clash with modern living environments, leading to conflicts and challenges. However, by acknowledging and accommodating these natural tendencies, pet owners can create environments that respect the animal's innate needs while maintaining harmony in the household. This might involve enriching the environment with toys, activities, and spaces that cater to instinctual behaviors, such as scratching posts for cats or puzzle feeders for dogs.

The study of instinct in animal behavior is a dynamic and evolving field, continually providing new insights into how animals think, feel, and act. Staying informed about these developments can enhance our understanding and improve our relationships with our pets. Whether it's through observing wild relatives, engaging with scientific research, or simply paying close attention to our pets' behaviors, we can gain a deeper appreciation for the powerful role that instinct plays in their lives.

Instinct is a fundamental aspect of animal behavior, shaping actions and reactions in ways that ensure survival and well-being. By understanding and respecting these innate behaviors, pet owners can create environments that support their pets' natural tendencies while fostering strong, positive relationships. Recognizing the roots of behaviors such as hunting, social hierarchy, maternal care, and communication helps in managing and enriching the lives of pets, ensuring they thrive in our care. Through empathy, observation, and informed care, we can honor the instinctual heritage of our pets and enjoy a harmonious and fulfilling companionship.

Migration Patterns and Their Causes

Migration is an astounding phenomenon observed across various animal species, where individuals travel from one region to another, often covering vast distances. This behavior is driven by multiple factors and is crucial for survival, reproduction, and the overall health of ecosystems. Understanding these migration patterns and their underlying causes can provide valuable insights into animal behavior and help in the conservation of many species.

One of the most well-documented examples of migration is that of birds. Many bird species migrate seasonally, traveling from breeding grounds in temperate regions to wintering grounds in the tropics. This seasonal migration is primarily driven by the availability of food and suitable breeding conditions. For example, the Arctic Tern undertakes an extraordinary journey from its breeding grounds in the Arctic to its wintering grounds in Antarctica, covering over 25,000 miles annually. This journey ensures that the birds have access to abundant food resources and optimal breeding conditions, increasing their chances of survival and reproductive success.

Similarly, monarch butterflies in North America embark on a remarkable migration, traveling thousands of miles from Canada and the United States to central Mexico. This migration is driven by the need to escape harsh winter conditions and find suitable overwintering sites. The butterflies rely on environmental cues such as temperature and daylight to time their migration, ensuring they arrive at their destination when conditions are favorable. This journey is so critical that it spans multiple generations, with butterflies laying eggs along the way, and their offspring continuing the journey.

Marine animals also exhibit fascinating migration patterns. Humpback whales, for instance, migrate from their feeding grounds in polar regions to breeding grounds in tropical and subtropical waters. These migrations are primarily driven by the need to exploit seasonal food resources and provide a safe environment for giving birth and raising their young. The journey is perilous, with whales facing threats from predation, ship strikes, and changing ocean conditions. Despite these challenges, the drive to migrate is deeply ingrained in their behavior, ensuring the survival of their species.

The migration of caribou in the Arctic is another compelling example. These large herbivores travel hundreds of miles between their summer and winter ranges, driven by the need to find food and avoid predators. During the summer, caribou move to the tundra where they can feed on fresh vegetation, while in the winter, they migrate to forested areas that provide shelter and access to lichens. This migration is essential for their survival and has significant impacts on the ecosystems they traverse, influencing plant growth and the distribution of other animals.

Fish species, such as salmon, also exhibit remarkable migratory behaviors. Salmon are anadromous, meaning they are born in freshwater rivers, migrate to the ocean to grow and mature, and then return to their natal rivers to spawn. This migration is driven by the need to find suitable spawning habitats and abundant food resources in the ocean. The journey upstream can be incredibly challenging, with fish navigating obstacles such as dams, predators, and strong currents. Despite these difficulties, the instinctual urge to return to their birthplace to reproduce is a powerful force that drives their migration.

Migration is not limited to long-distance journeys. Some animals exhibit altitudinal migration, moving between different elevations in response to seasonal changes. For example, many ungulates, such as elk and mountain goats, migrate to higher elevations in the summer to access lush alpine meadows and descend to lower elevations in the winter to avoid deep snow and find forage. This type of migration allows animals to exploit different habitats and resources throughout the year, enhancing their chances of survival.

Several factors drive migration, including environmental cues, genetic programming, and learned behaviors. Changes in temperature, photoperiod, and food availability are critical environmental triggers that signal the time to migrate. For instance, birds are known to use the position of the sun, stars, and the Earth's magnetic field to navigate during their long journeys. Genetic programming also plays a significant role, with many species having an innate drive to migrate that is passed down through generations. Additionally, some animals learn migratory routes and behaviors from their parents or social groups, ensuring the transfer of knowledge and increasing the success of future migrations. activities have a profound impact on migration patterns. Habitat destruction, climate change, and barriers such as roads and dams can disrupt traditional migratory routes and pose significant challenges to migrating animals. For example, the construction of dams on rivers can block the passage of migratory fish, preventing them from reaching their spawning grounds. Similarly, deforestation and urban development can fragment habitats, making it difficult for animals to find suitable stopover sites during their migration. Conservation efforts are crucial to mitigate these impacts and protect migratory species. Establishing wildlife corridors, removing barriers, and preserving critical habitats are essential strategies to support migration and ensure the survival of these species.

Migration also has significant ecological implications. Migratory animals play vital roles in their ecosystems, contributing to nutrient cycling, seed dispersal, and predator-prey dynamics. For example, the migration of wildebeest in the Serengeti contributes to the health of grasslands by grazing and fertilizing the soil with their droppings. Similarly, migratory birds can transport seeds and pollinate plants, facilitating the spread of plant species and maintaining biodiversity. The loss or disruption of migration can have cascading effects on ecosystems, highlighting the importance of preserving these natural phenomena.

In addition to ecological benefits, migration holds cultural and economic significance for human societies. Many indigenous communities have deep cultural connections to migratory species, relying on them for food, clothing, and spiritual practices. For example, the migration of caribou is central to the livelihoods and traditions of Arctic indigenous peoples. Moreover, migratory animals, such as birds and whales, attract tourists, supporting local economies and raising awareness about the importance of conservation.

Technological advancements have enhanced our understanding of migration patterns. Tools such as satellite tracking, GPS collars, and genetic analysis have provided valuable data on the movements and behaviors of migratory animals. For example, researchers can now track the precise routes and stopover sites of migratory birds, identifying critical habitats and potential threats. This information is essential for developing effective conservation strategies and ensuring the protection of migratory species.

Public awareness and education play a crucial role in supporting migration conservation efforts. By understanding the importance of migration and the challenges faced by migratory species, individuals can contribute to conservation initiatives. Simple actions, such as supporting habitat preservation, reducing pollution, and participating in citizen science projects, can make a significant difference. Engaging communities in conservation efforts fosters a sense of stewardship and responsibility towards migratory species and their habitats.

Migration patterns are a testament to the resilience and adaptability of animals. The journeys undertaken by migratory species are awe-inspiring, driven by a combination of environmental cues, genetic programming, and learned behaviors. These migrations are essential for survival, reproduction, and the health of ecosystems. However, human activities pose significant challenges to migration, highlighting the need for conservation efforts to protect these natural phenomena. By understanding and supporting migration, we can ensure the continued existence of these remarkable journeys and the species that undertake them.

Survival Strategies: Predation and Defense

Survival in the natural world often hinges on the delicate balance between predator and prey. For many species, the ability to evade predators and defend themselves is a matter of life and death. Understanding the myriad strategies animals employ to avoid becoming prey can offer fascinating insights into the complexities of ecological interactions and evolutionary adaptations. These survival strategies are shaped by the constant pressure to stay one step ahead in the deadly game of hide and seek that defines much of the animal kingdom.

Camouflage is one of the most common and effective defense mechanisms. By blending into their surroundings, animals can avoid detection by predators. This strategy, known as cryptic coloration, can be observed in numerous species. The peppered moth, for instance, blends seamlessly with the bark of trees, making it nearly invisible to birds. Similarly, the leaf-tailed gecko's body mimics the appearance of leaves, complete with intricate patterns and colors, allowing it to vanish into the foliage. Some animals take this a step further by altering their appearance according to their environment, such as the chameleon, which can change its skin color to match its surroundings.

Mimicry is another fascinating survival strategy. Some species evolve to resemble other, often more dangerous or unpalatable organisms. This can deter predators from attacking. The viceroy butterfly, for instance, closely resembles the toxic monarch butterfly. Predators that have learned to avoid the monarch due to its bitter taste and toxic properties will also steer clear of the viceroy. This form of mimicry, known as Batesian mimicry, relies on the predator's prior experience with the model species. In contrast, Mullerian mimicry involves two or more harmful species evolving to look similar, thereby reinforcing the avoidance behavior in predators.

Behavioral adaptations also play a crucial role in defense against predation. Many animals employ distraction displays or feign injury to lure predators away from their nests or young. The killdeer bird, for example, performs a "broken-wing" act to draw potential threats away from its nest. By pretending to be an easy target, it leads predators on a chase, ultimately steering them away from its vulnerable eggs or chicks. Another behavioral strategy is mobbing, where prey species collectively harass and drive away a predator. Birds, such as crows and small songbirds, often engage in mobbing to protect themselves and their offspring from larger predators like hawks or owls.

Chemical defenses are another ingenious method of deterring predators. Many insects, amphibians, and even some mammals produce noxious substances that make them unpalatable or toxic. The poison dart frog, with its bright colors, advertises its toxicity to potential predators. These frogs secrete potent toxins through their skin, which can cause serious harm or even death to any animal that attempts to eat them. Similarly, the bombardier beetle has a unique defense mechanism where it ejects a hot, noxious chemical spray from its abdomen when threatened. This rapid chemical reaction can burn and disorient predators, providing the beetle with a chance to escape.

Physical adaptations for defense are also widespread in the animal kingdom. Armoreddefenses, such as the hard shells of turtles and armadillos, provide a formidable barrier against predators. When threatened, these animals can retract their vulnerable parts, leaving only the tough exterior exposed. Porcupines, on the other hand, rely on their sharp quills to deter predators. When threatened, they raise their quills, which can easily embed into the skin of an attacker, causing pain and discouraging further pursuit.

Speed and agility are vital for many prey species. The ability to outrun or outmaneuver a predator can mean the difference between life and death. Gazelles, for instance, are known for their incredible speed and agility, which they use to evade predators like cheetahs. Their erratic, high-speed running patterns make it difficult for predators to predict their movements. Similarly, fish often rely on rapid, darting movements to escape from larger aquatic predators. Schools of fish can also confuse predators by moving in coordinated, swirling patterns, making it hard for the predator to single out an individual.

Social living can enhance the survival of prey species through collective vigilance and defense. Many animals form groups that provide safety in numbers. Herds of deer, flocks of birds, and schools of fish all benefit from the increased detection of predators. When one individual senses danger, it can alert the entire group, giving everyone a better chance to escape. This principle is known as the "many eyes" hypothesis. Additionally, some species engage in cooperative defense, where group members work together to fend off predators. Meerkats, for example, have designated sentinels that keep watch for danger while others forage, ready to sound the alarm if a predator approaches.

Aposematism, or warning coloration, is a strategy where animals use bright and conspicuous colors to signal their toxicity or unpalatability to potential predators. This form of honest signaling is seen in many species, such as the bright yellow and black stripes of bees and wasps, which warn predators of their painful sting. Similarly, the striking patterns of the coral snake serve as a clear warning of its venomous bite. Predators that have learned to associate these colors with danger are less likely to attack, providing the brightly colored species with a significant survival advantage.

Some animals have evolved to use deception as a means of defense. False eyespots, for instance, can confuse or scare predators. Many butterflies and moths have large, eye-like patterns on their wings that can startle or mislead predators into thinking they are facing a much larger animal. Similarly, some fish have eyespots near their tails, which can trick predators into attacking the less vital rear end, allowing the fish to escape.

In addition to these direct defense mechanisms, some prey species engage in indirect strategies to avoid predation. Habitat selection and use of cover can significantly reduce the risk of being detected by predators. Animals that live in dense vegetation, burrows, or other concealed environments are less likely to be seen and attacked. For example, rabbits use their burrows not only for shelter but also as a means to evade predators. By staying close to cover, they can quickly retreat to safety when threatened.

Finally, learning and memory play crucial roles in the survival strategies of many species. Animals that can learn from their experiences and remember the locations of predators or safe refuges have a better chance of surviving future encounters. Many birds, for instance, learn to recognize and avoid areas where they have previously encountered predators. Similarly, prey animals that have survived predator attacks often become more cautious and vigilant, increasing their chances of survival in the future.

The interplay between predation and defense is a dynamic and ongoing arms race, driving the evolution of a wide array of fascinating adaptations. These strategies, whether physical, chemical, behavioral, or social, illustrate the incredible ingenuity of nature in the face of constant threats. By studying these survival mechanisms, we gain a deeper appreciation for the complexity of ecological relationships and the relentless drive for survival that shapes the natural world.

Mating Rituals and Reproductive Behaviors

Mating rituals and reproductive behaviors in the animal kingdom exhibit an astonishing diversity, shaped by millions of years of evolution. These behaviors not only ensure the continuation of species but also play a crucial role in maintaining genetic diversity and adaptability. From elaborate courtship displays to intricate nest-building practices, the strategies animals use to attract mates and reproduce are as varied as the species themselves.

One of the most captivating examples of mating rituals is the courtship dance of birds of paradise. Found primarily in New Guinea and surrounding islands, these birds are famous for their spectacular plumage and intricate dances. Male birds of paradise perform elaborate displays, involving complex movements, vivid colors, and unique sounds, to attract females. These displays are not only a show of physical prowess but also signal the male's genetic fitness. Females carefully evaluate these performances, selecting mates based on the quality and intricacy of their displays. This selective process drives the evolution of increasingly elaborate and beautiful courtship behaviors.

In the marine world, the seahorse presents a fascinating case of reproductive behavior. Unique among fish, seahorses exhibit a form of male pregnancy. During courtship, the female transfers her eggs into a specialized pouch on the male's abdomen. The male then fertilizes the eggs internally and carries them until they hatch. This role reversal in parental care is rare and highlights the diverse strategies animals have evolved to ensure the survival of their offspring.

Insects, too, demonstrate a wide array of mating behaviors. The dance of the honeybee, known as the waggle dance, is a complex behavior used by scout bees to communicate the location of food sources to their hive mates. However, during the mating season, drones (male bees) participate in mating flights. They gather in specific areas known as drone congregation areas, where they compete to mate with virgin queens. The competition is fierce, and only the strongest and fastest drones succeed in mating, ensuring that only the fittest genes are passed on to the next generation.

Amphibians, such as frogs and toads, often rely on vocalizations to attract mates. During the breeding season, male frogs congregate in large groups near water bodies and produce loud, distinctive calls. Each species has a unique call, which females use to locate and select potential mates. The intensity and frequency of these calls can indicate the male's health and genetic quality, influencing female choice. This vocal competition can lead to choruses so loud that they can be heard from miles away, a testament to the importance of these calls in amphibian reproduction.

In the mammalian world, the rutting season of deer showcases another form of dramatic reproductive behavior. During this period, males engage in intense battles for dominance and the right to mate with females. These battles involve antler clashes and displays of strength and endurance. The victorious males earn the privilege to mate, while the defeated ones often retreat to recover and try again. This rutting behavior ensures that only the strongest and most capable males pass on their genes.

Fish often employ unique strategies to ensure reproductive success. The male stickleback, for instance, engages in elaborate nest-building behavior. Using plant material and secretions, he constructs a nest on the substrate of a water body. He then performs a series of courtship displays to attract a female to his nest. If she is impressed, she will enter the nest and lay her eggs, which the male then fertilizes. He guards the nest diligently, protecting the eggs from predators and ensuring their survival until they hatch.

Reptiles, such as the green anole lizard, use visual displays to attract mates and establish territory. Male green anoles have a brightly colored dewlap, a flap of skin beneath their throat, which they extend and display during courtship. They also perform push-up displays and head-bobbing to signal their presence and fitness to females. These behaviors serve both to attract mates and to deter rival males, ensuring that the strongest individuals have the best chance of reproducing.

In the insect world, the mating behavior of praying mantises is both fascinating and perilous. Female mantises are known for their aggressive behavior during and after mating, sometimes resorting to sexual cannibalism, where they consume the male. This behavior, though seemingly brutal, can provide the female with essential nutrients that support egg production. Males, aware of this risk, approach females cautiously and attempt to mate quickly to avoid becoming a meal.

Among mammals, the courtship and mating behavior of elephants is a complex and prolonged process. Male elephants, or bulls, enter a state called musth, characterized by increased testosterone levels and heightened aggression. During this period, bulls compete for access to females, engaging in physical confrontations to establish dominance. Female elephants, or cows, are choosy and often select mates based on the size and strength of the bulls, ensuring that their offspring inherit desirable traits. The bonds formed during these interactions can influence social structures within elephant herds, as dominant bulls often sire multiple calves.

In the avian world, the mating dances of cranes are a sight to behold. Cranes perform synchronized dances that include bowing, jumping, and wing flapping. These dances not only serve as courtship displays but also strengthen pair bonds between mates. Cranes are typically monogamous, and these dances help maintain the pair's connection throughout the breeding season. The intricate choreography of crane dances showcases the importance of communication and coordination in avian reproductive behavior.

One of the most extreme examples of reproductive behavior can be found in the deep sea, where anglerfish exhibit a unique form of sexual parasitism. In some species, the much smaller male anglerfish attaches himself to the female, fusing with her body and becoming entirely dependent on her for nutrients. This attachment ensures that the male's sperm is always available to fertilize the female's eggs, a crucial adaptation in the sparse and dark environment of the deep ocean.

In many species, parental care plays a crucial role in the survival of offspring. The emperor penguin, for instance, demonstrates remarkable dedication to parental duty. After the female lays a single egg, she transfers it to the male, who balances it on his feet and covers it with a flap of skin to keep it warm. The male endures the harsh Antarctic winter, fasting for months while protecting the egg. Once the egg hatches, the female returns with food, and both parents take turns caring for the chick. This cooperative parenting strategy ensures the survival of the vulnerable young in one of the most extreme environments on Earth.

The diversity of mating rituals and reproductive behaviors across the animal kingdom highlights the incredible adaptability and creativity of life. These behaviors are shaped by the constant pressures of natural selection, driving species to develop unique and often elaborate strategies to ensure their genetic legacy. From dazzling displays and intense battles to intricate dances and dedicated parental care, the ways in which animals attract mates and reproduce are as varied as the environments they inhabit. Understanding these behaviors not only provides insight into the lives of animals but also deepens our appreciation for the complexity and wonder of the natural world.

Communication Methods Among Wildlife

The natural world is teeming with diverse forms of communication among wildlife. These communication methods are vital for survival, aiding in everything from finding food to avoiding predators, and from establishing territories to forming social bonds. Animals have evolved a fascinating array of ways to convey information, relying on visual signals, auditory calls, chemical cues, and tactile interactions.

Visual signals are among the most conspicuous forms of wildlife communication. Many species use body language, coloration, and movement to convey messages. For instance, the vibrant plumage of male peacocks is not merely for show; it is a crucial part of their courtship ritual. The males fan out their iridescent tail feathers to create a dazzling display that attracts females.

This visual spectacle is a signal of the male's fitness, indicating his health and genetic quality.

Similarly, cuttlefish are masters of visual communication. These cephalopods can change their skin color and texture in an instant, using this ability to camouflage themselves, ward off predators, or signal potential mates. During courtship, male cuttlefish display striking patterns and colors to attract females. This dynamic use of visual signals highlights the importance of adaptability and precision in animal communication.

Auditory communication is another prevalent method among wildlife. Birds are perhaps the most well-known users of sound to communicate. Their songs serve multiple purposes, from attracting mates to marking territory. Each species has its own distinct song, and within species, individual birds can have unique variations. This complexity allows birds to convey a wealth of information through their calls. For example, the nightingale's song is renowned for its beauty and complexity, with males singing elaborate melodies to woo females and assert dominance over other males.

In the dense forests of Central and South America, howler monkeys use loud, resonant calls to communicate over long distances. These vocalizations serve to establish territory and maintain group cohesion. The calls are so powerful that they can be heard from several miles away, ensuring that other groups of howler monkeys are aware of their presence. This long-distance communication is crucial in the dense jungle environment where visibility is limited.

Chemical communication, or chemoreception, is another vital form of interaction among wildlife. Many animals rely on scent to communicate, marking their territories or signaling reproductive status. For instance, wolves use scent marking to define their territory. They urinate on trees, rocks, and bushes, leaving behind chemical markers that convey information about their identity and reproductive status. These scent marks help to prevent conflicts with other packs and ensure that the territory remains defended.

In the insect world, pheromones play a crucial role in communication. Ants use pheromones to create complex trails that guide their colony mates to food sources. When a foraging ant discovers food, it releases a pheromone trail on its way back to the nest. Other ants detect this chemical trail and follow it to the food. This efficient system ensures that the colony can exploit food resources effectively. Additionally, pheromones are used for alarm signaling, mating, and coordinating colony activities.

Tactile communication, though less conspicuous than visual or auditory signals, is equally important in the animal kingdom. Social insects like bees and ants use touch to convey information. Honeybees, for example, perform a "waggle dance" to communicate the location of food sources to their hive mates. The bee moves in a figure-eight pattern, with the direction and duration of the dance indicating the direction and distance of the food. This tactile form of communication is crucial for the survival of the hive, as it ensures that bees can efficiently gather nectar and pollen.

Primates, including humans, also rely heavily on tactile communication. Grooming is a common behavior among primates that serves to strengthen social bonds, reduce tension, and convey reassurance. In chimpanzee communities, grooming is a critical part of social life. It helps to establish and maintain alliances, resolve conflicts, and reinforce hierarchies. The physical act of grooming releases endorphins, promoting a sense of well-being and group cohesion.

Marine animals, living in the vast and often dark ocean, have evolved unique ways to communicate. Dolphins, for instance, use a combination of clicks, whistles, and body language to convey information. Their echolocation abilities allow them to navigate and hunt in murky waters, while their whistles are used for social communication. Each dolphin has a unique signature whistle that acts like a name, allowing individuals to recognize and call each other. This sophisticated system of vocal and non-vocal communication highlights the intelligence and social complexity of these marine mammals.

Whales, too, rely on sound to communicate over vast distances. Humpback whales are famous for their complex songs, which can last for hours and travel hundreds of miles underwater. These songs are believed to play a role in mating, with males singing to attract females and establish dominance. The songs are passed down through generations, with whales in different geographic regions developing distinct dialects.

In the realm of reptiles, communication often involves a combination of visual and chemical signals. Male lizards, such as the green anole, use bright coloration and display behaviors to communicate with rivals and potential mates. They perform push-ups and extend their dewlap, a colorful throat fan, to signal their presence and fitness. In addition to these visual displays, lizards also use chemical cues to mark their territory and signal reproductive status. These combined signals help to reduce conflicts and ensure successful mating.

Amphibians, like frogs and toads, primarily use vocalizations for communication. During the breeding season, male frogs gather in large groups and produce loud calls to attract females. Each species has a unique call, which helps females locate and select mates. The intensity and frequency of these calls can indicate the male's health and genetic quality. In some species, males also use visual signals, such as inflating their vocal sacs, to enhance their calls and attract females.

Even within the same species, animals may use multiple forms of communication to convey different types of information. For example, elephants use a combination of vocalizations, body language, and chemical signals to communicate. They produce low-frequency rumbles that can travel long distances, allowing them to stay in contact with herd members even when they are far apart. Elephants also use touch and scent to reinforce social bonds and convey reproductive status. This multimodal communication system reflects the complex social structure of elephant herds and their need to coordinate activities across large distances.

Understanding the diverse communication methods among wildlife not only provides insight into the lives of animals but also highlights the intricate and interconnected nature of ecosystems. Each form of communication has evolved to suit the specific needs and environments of different species, demonstrating the adaptability and ingenuity of life on Earth. By studying these communication strategies, we can gain a deeper appreciation for the complexity of animal behavior and the delicate balance of natural systems.

Chapter 3: Factors Influencing Animal Behavior

Genetic and Inherited Traits

Genetic and inherited traits are the blueprints that dictate the physical and behavioral characteristics of organisms, shaping their survival and adaptation strategies. These traits are passed from one generation to the next through genes, which are segments of DNA containing the instructions for building and maintaining living organisms. Understanding genetics and inheritance is crucial for unraveling the complexities of life, from the simplest bacteria to the most complex mammals.

Genes are the fundamental units of heredity, located on chromosomes within the cell nucleus. Each gene consists of a specific sequence of DNA that encodes for a particular protein or set of proteins. These proteins perform essential functions in the body, influencing traits such as eye color, height, and susceptibility to diseases. The combination of genes inherited from both parents determines an individual's genotype, which in turn influences their phenotype—the observable characteristics.

One of the most striking examples of inherited traits is seen in the coat colors and patterns of domestic animals. For instance, the diverse coat colors in dogs are a result of variations in just a few genes. The gene responsible for coat color can have several different versions, or alleles, which interact in complex ways to produce the wide range of colors and patterns seen in dog breeds. Similarly, in cats, the gene for coat color can lead to tabby, solid, or spotted patterns, depending on the specific alleles present.

Mendelian inheritance, named after Gregor Mendel, the father of genetics, describes how traits are transmitted from parents to offspring through dominant and recessive alleles. Mendel's experiments with pea plants in the 19th century revealed that traits are inherited in predictable patterns. For example, in pea plants, the allele for purple flowers is dominant over the allele for white flowers. When a plant inherits one purple allele and one white allele, the purple trait is expressed in the phenotype. However, if a plant inherits two white alleles, the white trait is expressed.

Beyond Mendelian inheritance, many traits are influenced by multiple genes and environmental factors. These complex traits, such as height, intelligence, and behavior, do not follow simple dominant-recessive patterns. Instead, they result from the interplay of numerous genes and their interactions with environmental influences. For example, human height is determined by hundreds of genes, each contributing a small effect, along with factors such as nutrition and overall health.

The study of genetic inheritance extends to understanding inherited diseases and disorders. Genetic mutations—changes in the DNA sequence—can lead to various inherited conditions. Some mutations are harmless, while others can cause serious health problems. For instance, cystic fibrosis is a genetic disorder caused by a mutation in the CFTR gene. This mutation leads to the production of a faulty protein that affects the respiratory and digestive systems. Cystic fibrosis follows a recessive inheritance pattern, meaning that an individual must inherit two copies of the mutated gene (one from each parent) to develop the disease.

Genetic counseling is an important field that helps individuals and families understand their genetic makeup and the risks of inherited conditions. Genetic counselors provide information about the likelihood of passing on genetic disorders, the availability of genetic testing, and the options for managing or preventing these conditions. For example, couples with a family history of genetic disorders may seek genetic counseling to assess the risk of having a child with a particular condition and to explore reproductive options such as preimplantation genetic diagnosis (PGD) or adoption.

Selective breeding, or artificial selection, is a practice that has been used for centuries to enhance desirable traits in plants and animals. By choosing individuals with specific traits to reproduce, humans have been able to shape the characteristics of domesticated species. For example, farmers have selectively bred crops to improve yield, disease resistance, and nutritional content. Similarly, livestock breeders have selected animals for traits such as faster growth, higher milk production, and better meat quality. Selective breeding has led to significant advancements in agriculture and animal husbandry, but it also raises ethical considerations regarding animal welfare and genetic diversity.

In the natural world, evolutionary processes drive the inheritance and variation of traits. Natural selection, a key mechanism of evolution, favors individuals with traits that enhance their survival and reproductive success in a given environment. Over time, these advantageous traits become more common in the population. For example, the long necks of giraffes are thought to have evolved through natural selection, as individuals with longer necks could reach higher foliage and had a better chance of surviving and reproducing. This gradual accumulation of beneficial traits leads to the adaptation of species to their environments.

Genetic diversity is crucial for the health and resilience of populations. A diverse gene pool provides a wide range of traits that can help populations adapt to changing environments and resist diseases. Conservation efforts often focus on preserving genetic diversity to ensure the long-term survival of endangered species. For example, breeding programs for endangered animals, such as the California condor, aim to maintain genetic diversity by carefully managing the mating of individuals to avoid inbreeding and promote healthy populations.

Advances in genetic research have revolutionized our understanding of inherited traits and opened new possibilities for medicine and biotechnology. The Human Genome Project, completed in 2003, mapped the entire human genome, providing a comprehensive blueprint of our genetic makeup. This monumental achievement has paved the way for personalized medicine, where treatments can be tailored to an individual's genetic profile. For instance, certain cancers can be treated more effectively by targeting specific genetic mutations present in the tumor cells.

Genetic engineering is another groundbreaking field that allows scientists to modify the genetic material of organisms. By inserting, deleting, or altering specific genes, researchers can create organisms with desired traits. This technology has numerous applications, from developing crops that are resistant to pests and diseases to producing insulin for diabetes treatment. However, genetic engineering also raises ethical and environmental concerns, such as the potential for unintended consequences and the impact on biodiversity.

Epigenetics is an emerging field that explores how environmental factors can influence gene expression without changing the underlying DNA sequence. Epigenetic modifications, such as DNA methylation and histone modification, can turn genes on or off, affecting an individual's phenotype. These changes can be influenced by factors such as diet, stress, and exposure to toxins. For example, studies have shown that maternal nutrition during pregnancy can affect the health and development of offspring through epigenetic mechanisms. Epigenetics adds another layer of complexity to our understanding of inheritance and highlights the dynamic interplay between genes and the environment.

In conclusion, genetic and inherited traits form the foundation of life, shaping the diversity and adaptability of organisms. From the intricate patterns of inheritance described by Mendel to the complex interactions of multiple genes and environmental factors, the study of genetics provides profound insights into the mechanisms of life. As our knowledge of genetics continues to expand, we are poised to unlock new possibilities for improving health, agriculture, and conservation, while also grappling with the ethical and environmental implications of these advancements.

Environmental Influences and Adaptations

Environmental influences shape the survival strategies and adaptations of organisms, molding them into the remarkable forms we observe today. Every niche on Earth, from the deepest oceans to the highest mountains, presents unique challenges. The pressure to survive in these diverse environments drives organisms to develop specialized traits and behaviors, ensuring their continued existence.

Adaptation, an evolutionary process, allows organisms to become better suited to their habitats. These adaptations can be structural, physiological, or behavioral, and they often result from the interplay between genetics and environmental pressures. For instance, the thick fur of Arctic foxes is a structural adaptation that helps them survive frigid temperatures, while their ability to change fur color with the seasons is a behavioral adaptation that provides camouflage in both snowy and tundra landscapes.

One of the most iconic examples of adaptation is the Galápagos finches studied by Charles Darwin. These finches, residing on different islands, exhibit variations in beak shape and size, each suited to their specific dietary needs. Finches that feed on large seeds have robust, thick beaks capable of cracking tough shells, whereas those that consume insects have slender, pointed beaks ideal for probing crevices. This divergence in beak morphology illustrates how environmental demands can drive the evolution of distinct adaptations within a species.

Plants, too, exhibit remarkable adaptations to their environments. Cacti, native to arid deserts, have evolved to minimize water loss through features like thick, fleshy stems that store water and spines that reduce air flow and shade the plant. Their shallow, widespread root systems quickly absorb any available moisture. In contrast, mangrove trees thrive in saline coastal environments with their unique root systems that filter salt and stabilize the shoreline against erosion. These adaptations enable mangroves to survive and flourish where most other plant species would perish.

Extreme environments often elicit some of the most fascinating adaptations. Deep-sea organisms, for instance, live in total darkness under immense pressure. Many have evolved bioluminescence, the ability to produce light through chemical reactions, which they use for communication, attracting mates, or luring prey. The anglerfish, with its luminescent lure, is a prime example. This appendage dangles in front of the fish's mouth, attracting unsuspecting prey in the pitch-black depths.

Desert animals, facing intense heat and scarce water, display a variety of adaptations to conserve hydration and regulate body temperature. The fennec fox, with its enormous ears, dissipates heat effectively and can survive on minimal water. Meanwhile, the kangaroo rat can live its entire life without drinking water, deriving moisture solely from its food. These physiological and behavioral adaptations are crucial for survival in such harsh conditions.

Seasonal changes also spur adaptations. Many animals undergo hibernation or migration to cope with fluctuating resources and temperatures. Bears, for example, enter a state of torpor during winter, significantly lowering their metabolism to conserve energy. Birds like the Arctic tern embark on long migrations, traveling from polar regions to the equator and back, exploiting seasonal abundance in different parts of the world. These strategies ensure that organisms remain active and reproductive despite seasonal constraints. activity has become a significant environmental influence, prompting adaptations in various species. Urban environments, with their unique challenges, have led to the emergence of urban-adapted traits in animals. Pigeons, originally cliff dwellers, have adapted to cityscapes by nesting on buildings and feeding on human-provided food sources. Similarly, some plants have evolved to thrive in polluted soils, developing mechanisms to tolerate heavy metals or other contaminants.

Climate change, a pressing global issue, is driving rapid adaptations in many species as they struggle to cope with shifting conditions. Some species are altering their geographic ranges, moving to cooler areas as temperatures rise. The American pika, a small mammal adapted to cold alpine climates, is moving to higher elevations in response to warming temperatures. However, not all species can migrate, and those that cannot may face extinction if they cannot adapt quickly enough.

Adaptations are not always perfect solutions; they often involve trade-offs. For instance, the long neck of a giraffe allows it to reach high foliage but also requires a specialized cardiovascular system to pump blood to its brain. Similarly, the streamlined bodies of fish enable efficient swimming but limit their ability to maneuver in tight spaces. These trade-offs highlight the complex balance organisms must strike to thrive in their environments.

The role of plasticity—the ability of an organism to change its phenotype in response to environmental conditions—is critical in understanding adaptations. Phenotypic plasticity allows individuals to adjust their behavior, physiology, or morphology within their lifetime, providing a flexible response to environmental variability. For example, some fish can alter their sex based on the social environment, ensuring reproductive success when mates are scarce.

Humans, with their cultural and technological advancements, exhibit unique adaptations. Unlike other species, humans adapt to their environment through innovation. Clothing, shelter, and tools have allowed humans to inhabit virtually every corner of the globe. Cultural practices, such as agriculture and medicine, have transformed human-environment interactions, enabling population growth and societal development. However, these adaptations also pose challenges, such as environmental degradation and resource depletion.

Understanding the mechanisms behind environmental influences and adaptations is crucial for conservation efforts. Protecting habitats and maintaining biodiversity ensures that species retain the capacity to adapt to changing conditions. Conservation strategies often focus on preserving genetic diversity, which provides the raw material for adaptation. By safeguarding diverse ecosystems, we support the resilience of species and their ability to cope with future environmental changes.

In conclusion, the interplay between environmental influences and adaptations is a dynamic and intricate process that shapes the natural world. From the microevolution of Galápagos finches to the plasticity of human culture, the ability to adapt is a testament to the resilience and ingenuity of life. As we face unprecedented environmental challenges, understanding and supporting these adaptive processes will be essential for the survival and flourishing of both natural ecosystems and human societies. This ongoing dance between organisms and their environments reveals the beauty and complexity of life on Earth, underscoring the importance of preserving the delicate balance that sustains us all.

The Impact of Human Activities

Human activities have had profound impacts on the natural world, influencing ecosystems, climate, and biodiversity in ways that are both complex and far-reaching. From the dawn of agriculture to the industrial revolution and the digital age, our species has left an indelible mark on the environment, often with unintended consequences.

Agriculture, one of the earliest human activities to alter landscapes, has transformed forests, grasslands, and wetlands into croplands and pastures. This transformation has provided food and resources for growing populations but has also led to habitat loss, soil degradation, and water scarcity. The invention of irrigation and the use of fertilizers have increased crop yields but have also caused significant environmental impacts, such as salinization of soils and eutrophication of water bodies.

Deforestation, driven by the need for timber and agricultural land, is another critical impact of human activity. Forests, which are home to a vast array of species and act as carbon sinks, are being cleared at alarming rates. The Amazon rainforest, often referred to as the "lungs of the Earth," has seen significant deforestation due to cattle ranching, soy cultivation, and logging. This not only threatens biodiversity but also contributes to climate change by releasing stored carbon dioxide into the atmosphere.

Urbanization, the growth of cities and towns, has dramatically altered natural landscapes. As populations concentrate in urban areas, the demand for housing, infrastructure, and services increases. This leads to the conversion of natural habitats into built environments, reducing green spaces and fragmenting ecosystems. Urban sprawl often encroaches on wildlife habitats, leading to conflicts between humans and animals. Moreover, cities generate substantial amounts of waste and pollution, further impacting air, water, and soil quality.

Industrialization has been a double-edged sword for humanity. While it has brought unprecedented economic growth and technological advancement, it has also led to significant environmental degradation. Factories and power plants emit pollutants into the air and water, contributing to health problems and ecosystem damage. The burning of fossil fuels for energy releases greenhouse gases, which drive climate change. Industrial processes often involve the extraction of natural resources, leading to habitat destruction and the depletion of non-renewable resources.

Climate change, arguably the most pressing environmental issue of our time, is primarily driven by human activities. The burning of fossil fuels, deforestation, and various industrial processes release large amounts of greenhouse gases, such as carbon dioxide and methane, into the atmosphere. These gases trap heat, leading to global warming and associated climate changes. Rising temperatures affect weather patterns, sea levels, and the frequency and intensity of extreme weather events. This, in turn, impacts ecosystems, agriculture, water resources, and human health.

Pollution is another significant impact of human activities. Air pollution, caused by vehicle emissions, industrial discharges, and burning of biomass, leads to respiratory problems, cardiovascular diseases, and premature deaths. Water pollution, from agricultural runoff, industrial waste, and untreated sewage, contaminates drinking water sources and harms aquatic life. Soil pollution, resulting from the use of pesticides, heavy metals, and industrial chemicals, degrades land and affects food safety. Plastic pollution, a relatively recent but pervasive problem, affects oceans and marine life, as plastics take centuries to decompose.

Overexploitation of natural resources is a consequence of human consumption patterns. Fisheries, for example, are experiencing declines due to overfishing, threatening marine biodiversity and the livelihoods of communities that depend on fishing. The demand for wildlife products, such as ivory, rhino horn, and exotic pets, drives poaching and illegal trade, pushing many species towards extinction. Forests are logged unsustainably, and minerals and fossil fuels are extracted at rates that exceed the Earth's ability to replenish them. These practices not only deplete resources but also disrupt ecosystems and contribute to environmental degradation.

Loss of biodiversity is a significant consequence of human activities. Habitat destruction, pollution, climate change, and overexploitation are driving many species to the brink of extinction. Biodiversity loss affects ecosystem services that humans rely on, such as pollination, water purification, and disease regulation. It also reduces genetic diversity, which is crucial for species adaptation to changing conditions. The decline of keystone species, those that play critical roles in their ecosystems, can lead to cascading effects, further destabilizing ecosystems. activities have also led to the introduction of invasive species, which can outcompete, prey on, or bring diseases to native species. These invasions often result from global trade and travel, which transport species to new areas. Invasive species can alter habitats, reduce biodiversity, and disrupt ecosystem functions. For example, the introduction of the brown tree snake to Guam has led to the decline of native bird populations, while the spread of zebra mussels in North American waterways has impacted aquatic ecosystems and infrastructure.

Mitigating the impacts of human activities on the environment requires concerted efforts at individual, community, national, and global levels. Sustainable practices, such as reducing waste, conserving energy, and protecting natural habitats, are essential. Transitioning to renewable energy sources, like solar and wind, can reduce greenhouse gas emissions and reliance on fossil fuels. Implementing policies that promote conservation, sustainable resource use, and pollution control can help protect ecosystems and biodiversity.

Environmental education and awareness are crucial for fostering a culture of sustainability. By understanding the impacts of their actions, individuals can make informed choices that benefit the environment. Community initiatives, such as tree planting, clean-up drives, and local conservation projects, can have a positive impact. Governments and organizations play a key role in enforcing environmental regulations, supporting research and innovation, and promoting green technologies.

Restoration efforts are also vital for reversing some of the damage caused by human activities. Reforestation, wetland restoration, and the creation of protected areas can help restore ecosystems and provide habitat for wildlife. Rehabilitation of degraded lands and polluted sites can improve ecosystem services and human well-being. Conservation programs aimed at protecting endangered species and their habitats can prevent further biodiversity loss.

In conclusion, human activities have significantly impacted the environment, leading to habitat destruction, pollution, climate change, and biodiversity loss. Addressing these challenges requires a multifaceted approach that includes sustainable practices, policy measures, education, and restoration efforts. By understanding and mitigating our impacts, we can work towards a future where both humans and nature thrive. The choices we make today will determine the health of our planet for generations to come, emphasizing the importance of stewardship and responsible management of natural resources.

Learning and Experience in Animal Behavior

Animals exhibit a fascinating array of behaviors, many of which are shaped by a combination of learning and experience. From the moment they are born, animals interact with their environment and others of their kind, gathering knowledge that influences their survival and reproduction. Understanding how animals learn and adapt can offer profound insights into their lives and the complexity of their behaviors.

Learning in animals can be broadly categorized into several types: habituation, sensitization, classical conditioning, operant conditioning, and social learning. Each type plays a unique role in how animals perceive and respond to their environment.

Habituation is the simplest form of learning and involves an animal becoming less responsive to a repeated stimulus that has no positive or negative consequence. For example, birds may initially be startled by a scarecrow in a field, but as they repeatedly encounter it without any associated threat, they gradually ignore it. This process allows animals to conserve energy and attention for more significant stimuli.

Sensitization, in contrast, is an increased responsiveness to a stimulus following a strong or noxious experience. For instance, a dog that has been startled by a loud noise may become more alert and reactive to subsequent sounds. Sensitization can enhance an animal's ability to detect and respond to potential threats.

Classical conditioning, famously demonstrated by Ivan Pavlov's experiments with dogs, occurs when an animal learns to associate a neutral stimulus with a significant one. In Pavlov's case, dogs learned to associate the sound of a bell with the presentation of food, eventually salivating at the sound alone. This form of learning helps animals predict important events in their environment, such as the availability of food or the presence of danger.

Operant conditioning involves learning through consequences, where behaviors are shaped by rewards or punishments. B.F. Skinner's work with rats and pigeons highlighted this type of learning. Animals learn to repeat behaviors that lead to positive outcomes, such as receiving food, and avoid behaviors that result in negative outcomes, such as a shock. This type of learning is crucial for acquiring new skills and adapting to changing environments.

Social learning, or learning from others, is particularly important in the animal kingdom. Many animals observe and imitate the behaviors of their peers or parents. Young chimpanzees, for example, learn to use tools by watching their mothers. This transmission of knowledge ensures that successful behaviors are passed down through generations, enhancing the survival of the species.

Experience plays a crucial role in shaping animal behavior, often interacting with innate tendencies. For example, while many birds are born with an instinct to sing, the specific songs they produce are often influenced by listening to adult conspecifics. This blend of innate ability and learned experience ensures that the songs are both species-specific and adapted to local environments.

One of the most remarkable examples of learning and experience can be seen in migratory birds. These birds undertake long and perilous journeys between breeding and wintering grounds, often spanning thousands of miles. While they possess an innate ability to sense magnetic fields and use the stars for navigation, their success is heavily reliant on experience. Young birds typically follow older, more experienced individuals on their first migration, learning the routes and stopover sites essential for survival.

The role of play in learning is another fascinating aspect of animal behavior. Play allows young animals to practice and refine skills that are crucial in adulthood. Predator species like lions and wolves engage in play that mimics hunting behaviors, while social animals like dolphins and primates play games that build social bonds and communication skills. Through play, animals explore their physical capabilities, learn social rules, and develop problem-solving abilities.

Problem-solving and tool use are often highlighted as indicators of advanced learning and cognition in animals. Crows and ravens, for instance, are renowned for their ability to solve complex problems and use tools to obtain food. In one study, New Caledonian crows were observed crafting hooks from twigs to extract insects from tree bark. This sophisticated behavior demonstrates not only the ability to learn from experience but also to innovate and adapt to novel challenges.

Memory is a critical component of learning and experience in animal behavior. Many animals rely on memory to locate food sources, navigate their territories, and recognize individuals. Elephants, known for their impressive memory, can remember the locations of water holes and the faces of other elephants over many years. This ability is vital for their survival in the often harsh and variable environments they inhabit.

Communication, another complex behavior influenced by learning and experience, is essential for social animals. Many species rely on vocalizations, body language, and chemical signals to convey information. For example, bees perform intricate "waggle dances" to inform hive mates about the location of food sources. This dance is not an innate behavior but one that bees learn through experience and practice. Similarly, vervet monkeys have specific alarm calls for different predators, and young monkeys learn to associate these calls with the appropriate threats through observation and experience.

Learning and experience also play a pivotal role in mating behaviors and reproductive success. Many animals engage in elaborate courtship displays and rituals that are learned and refined through practice. Male bowerbirds, for instance, construct intricate structures decorated with colorful objects to attract females. The skill and creativity involved in building these bowers improve with experience, increasing the male's chances of reproductive success.

Parental care, another aspect of reproductive behavior, is often learned. In many bird species, for example, parents must learn how to feed and protect their young effectively. Experience improves their ability to provide for their offspring, enhancing the survival rates of their chicks. In mammals, maternal behaviors such as nursing and grooming are learned through both instinct and experience, ensuring that the young receive the care they need for healthy development.

Despite the impressive learning abilities of many animals, there are limits to what they can learn, often imposed by their neurological and physiological constraints. Different species have evolved to excel in different types of learning that best suit their ecological niches. For example, while rats are excellent at navigating mazes and solving problems related to food acquisition, they are not as adept at tasks that require advanced social learning, which primates excel in.

In conclusion, learning and experience are fundamental to animal behavior, influencing how animals interact with their environment, acquire necessary skills, and ensure their survival and reproduction. The intricate interplay between innate abilities and learned behaviors showcases the remarkable adaptability and complexity of the animal kingdom. Understanding these processes not only enriches our appreciation of animals but also provides valuable insights into the evolutionary mechanisms that drive behavior. By studying how animals learn and adapt, we continue to uncover the profound intelligence and resilience that characterize life on Earth.

Case Studies: Behavioral Changes Over Time

The transformation of animal behavior over time offers fascinating insights into the adaptability and complexity of the animal kingdom. Examining case studies of behavioral changes allows us to understand how animals respond to environmental pressures, social dynamics, and evolutionary demands. These changes can be subtle or dramatic, influenced by factors such as habitat alteration, climate change, human activity, and interspecies interactions.

One compelling case study involves the peppered moth (Bistonbetularia) in England. Before the Industrial Revolution, the majority of peppered moths were light-colored, which camouflaged them against the lichen-covered trees. However, as industrial pollution darkened the trees with soot, a darker variant of the moth became more common. This shift, known as industrial melanism, demonstrated a rapid evolutionary response to environmental change. Predation pressure from birds favored the survival of darker moths in polluted areas, leading to an increase in their population. This case exemplifies natural selection in action, highlighting how species can adapt their behavior and appearance in response to human-induced environmental changes.

Another notable example is the introduction of cane toads (Rhinella marina) to Australia in the 1930s. Originally brought in to control agricultural pests, cane toads quickly became an invasive species, spreading across the continent and causing significant ecological disruption. Native Australian predators, unfamiliar with the toxic toads, suffered population declines after consuming them. Over time, some native species, such as the black kite and the water monitor, began to exhibit behavioral changes, learning to avoid or safely handle the toads. These adaptations illustrate the ability of native species to develop new survival strategies in response to the introduction of invasive species.

The behavior of African elephants (Loxodonta africana) has also changed significantly due to human pressures. In areas with high levels of poaching, researchers have observed an increase in tuskless elephants, particularly among females. Poaching for ivory has exerted strong selective pressure, favoring individuals without tusks who are less likely to be targeted. This behavioral and physiological change underscores the profound impact of human activity on wildlife and how animals can adapt over generations to survive in altered environments.

Urbanization presents another context in which animal behavior changes over time. Urban environments create unique challenges and opportunities for wildlife. The red fox (Vulpes vulpes), for instance, has become adept at living in cities, exhibiting altered foraging behaviors and increased nocturnality to avoid human activity. Urban foxes often scavenge for food in garbage bins and have learned to navigate the complex cityscape. This adaptability demonstrates how animals can modify their behaviors to exploit new habitats created by human development.

Climate change is driving behavioral changes in many species as they adapt to shifting environmental conditions. The timing of migration in birds, for example, is altering in response to changing temperatures. The pied flycatcher (Ficedulahypoleuca) has been arriving earlier at its breeding grounds in Europe, synchronizing its migration with the earlier emergence of its insect prey. This adjustment is crucial for the birds to ensure adequate food supply for rearing their young. However, not all species can adapt quickly enough, leading to mismatches between life cycle events and environmental conditions, which can have detrimental effects on populations.

Social dynamics within species can also lead to behavioral changes over time. Among primates, the culture of tool use in chimpanzees (Pan troglodytes) is a well-documented example. Different groups of chimpanzees have developed unique techniques for using tools to obtain food, such as using sticks to extract termites or rocks to crack nuts. These behaviors are passed down through generations via social learning, resulting in distinct cultural traditions within populations. Changes in tool use can occur over time as new techniques are discovered and adopted, illustrating the dynamic nature of animal cultures.

The domestication of animals provides another rich field of study for behavioral changes. Dogs (Canis lupus familiaris), descended from wolves, have undergone significant behavioral and physiological transformations through domestication. Selective breeding for traits desirable to humans, such as docility and trainability, has resulted in a wide variety of dog breeds with specialized behaviors. The process of domestication illustrates how human intervention can drastically alter the behavior of a species over a relatively short evolutionary timespan.

In aquatic environments, changes in behavior due to human influence are also evident. Overfishing has led to shifts in the behavior of many fish species. For example, Atlantic cod (Gadusmorhua) have altered their reproductive strategies in response to intense fishing pressure. Cod now tend to spawn at smaller sizes and younger ages, a shift that has implications for the population dynamics and recovery of the species. These changes highlight the profound impact of human exploitation on marine life and the need for sustainable management practices.

Understanding behavioral changes over time is crucial for conservation efforts. By recognizing how animals adapt to environmental pressures, conservationists can develop strategies that support these adaptations. For instance, creating wildlife corridors can facilitate the movement of species in response to habitat fragmentation, allowing them to access new areas for feeding and breeding. Protecting critical habitats and reducing human-wildlife conflict are also essential for supporting the natural behavioral adaptations of species.

In studying behavioral changes, it is important to consider the role of plasticity—the ability of individuals to alter their behavior in response to environmental conditions. Behavioral plasticity allows animals to cope with immediate challenges and can be a precursor to longer-term evolutionary changes. For example, the ability of some bird species to adjust their song frequencies in noisy urban environments demonstrates behavioral plasticity. These changes enable birds to effectively communicate despite the presence of anthropogenic noise, enhancing their chances of successful reproduction.

Longitudinal studies, which track changes in behavior over extended periods, provide valuable insights into the processes underlying behavioral adaptations. Such studies can reveal patterns and trends that are not apparent in short-term observations. They can also identify the factors driving behavioral changes, whether they are genetic, environmental, or social. By examining these factors, researchers can better understand the mechanisms of adaptation and predict how species might respond to future challenges.

Behavioral changes over time are not limited to individual species but can also affect ecosystems and community dynamics. Changes in the behavior of keystone species, for example, can have cascading effects on entire ecosystems. Sea otters (Enhydra lutris), which prey on sea urchins, play a critical role in maintaining kelp forest ecosystems. Overhunting of sea otters led to an increase in sea urchin populations, resulting in the overgrazing of kelp forests. The reintroduction and recovery of sea otter populations have helped restore the balance in these ecosystems, demonstrating the interconnectedness of species and the importance of predator-prey relationships.

Behavioral changes over time reflect the dynamic and ever-evolving nature of the animal kingdom. These changes are driven by a complex interplay of environmental pressures, social interactions, and evolutionary processes. By studying these changes, we gain a deeper understanding of the resilience and adaptability of animals, insights that are crucial for conservation and the sustainable management of wildlife. The stories of peppered moths, cane toads, elephants, urban foxes, migratory birds, chimpanzees, domesticated dogs, and cod fish all illustrate the remarkable capacity of animals to adjust their behaviors in response to a changing world. These case studies underscore the importance of protecting biodiversity and supporting the natural processes that allow species to thrive in the face of adversity.

Chapter 4: Animal Behavior and Conservation

The Importance of Behavioral Research in Conservation

Behavioral research is a cornerstone of modern conservation efforts, providing critical insights into how animals interact with their environment, each other, and human activities. Understanding these behaviors is essential for developing effective conservation strategies that ensure the survival and well-being of species. This chapter delves into the importance of behavioral research, illustrating its role through various examples and explaining how it informs conservation practices.

The study of animal behavior, or ethology, offers a window into the lives of species, revealing patterns that can indicate the health and stability of populations. For instance, changes in foraging behavior can signal shifts in food availability or habitat quality. By monitoring these behaviors, conservationists can identify areas where intervention is necessary. One notable example is the foraging behavior of sea birds such as puffins. Puffins' diet primarily consists of fish, and their foraging success can be directly linked to the health of marine ecosystems. Behavioral studies have shown that when fish stocks decline due to overfishing or climate change, puffins travel greater distances and spend more time searching for food, which affects their breeding success. By understanding these behavioral changes, conservationists can advocate for fishing regulations and marine protected areas to ensure sustainable fish populations and support bird conservation.

Migration patterns are another vital aspect of behavioral research that informs conservation. Many species, from monarch butterflies to humpback whales, undertake long migrations that are crucial for their survival and reproduction. Disruptions to these migrations, whether from habitat loss, climate change, or human-made barriers, can have severe consequences. Researchers tracking the migratory routes of species like the Arctic tern, which travels from the Arctic to the Antarctic and back each year, provide essential data on the critical stopover points and breeding grounds that need protection. This information is invaluable for creating international conservation policies that ensure these routes remain viable.

Social behavior within animal communities also plays a significant role in conservation. Many species rely on complex social structures for breeding, foraging, and protection from predators. Elephants, for example, live in matriarchal societies where older females lead and transfer knowledge to younger generations. Disrupting these social structures, whether through poaching or habitat fragmentation, can have long-lasting effects on the population. Behavioral research has shown that orphaned elephants, who have lost their matriarchs, often exhibit signs of trauma and have difficulty integrating into new herds. This understanding has led to conservation programs that focus not only on protecting elephants but also on rehabilitating and reintegrating orphans into social groups.

Behavioral research is crucial for addressing human-wildlife conflicts, which are a growing challenge in conservation. As human populations expand and encroach on wildlife habitats, conflicts arise, often leading to negative outcomes for both people and animals. Studying the behavior of species involved in these conflicts can lead to more effective solutions. For example, in areas where elephants raid crops, researchers have discovered that elephants are deterred by bees. Implementing beehive fences around agricultural fields has proven to be a successful, non-lethal method for keeping elephants away from crops, benefiting both farmers and elephant populations.

The reproductive behavior of endangered species is another area where behavioral research is indispensable. For species with small populations, understanding their mating systems, courtship behaviors, and parental care is critical for successful breeding programs. The California condor, once on the brink of extinction, has been the focus of intensive behavioral studies to improve captive breeding efforts. Researchers observed that condors have complex social interactions and mate selection processes that are crucial for successful reproduction. By replicating these conditions in captivity, conservationists have been able to increase the number of condor chicks hatched and raised, contributing to the species' gradual recovery.

Behavioral research also informs habitat restoration efforts. Restoring degraded habitats to a state where they can support viable wildlife populations requires an understanding of the specific needs and behaviors of the target species. For example, in the restoration of wetland habitats for amphibians, researchers study the breeding and foraging behaviors of species like the red-legged frog. This knowledge helps in designing wetlands that provide the necessary conditions for these behaviors, ensuring the success of the restoration project and the survival of the species.

The study of animal behaviors can reveal early warning signs of environmental stress. Behavioral indicators, such as changes in feeding habits, increased aggression, or altered reproductive patterns, often precede more obvious signs of population decline. By monitoring these behaviors, conservationists can take proactive measures to mitigate threats before they result in significant population losses. In coral reef ecosystems, for example, the behavior of fish and other marine organisms can indicate the health of the reef. Changes in fish behavior, such as decreased activity or changes in territory, can signal the onset of coral bleaching or other stressors, prompting early intervention efforts.

The role of behavioral research in conservation extends to public education and engagement. Understanding and communicating the fascinating behaviors of wildlife can foster a greater appreciation for biodiversity and the need for conservation. Programs that involve the public in behavioral research, such as citizen science initiatives, can enhance conservation efforts by increasing data collection and raising awareness. Birdwatching programs, for instance, engage the public in monitoring bird behaviors and migrations, contributing valuable data to conservationists while fostering a connection between people and nature.

Behavioral research also plays a critical role in the development and implementation of wildlife corridors. These corridors are essential for maintaining genetic diversity and allowing species to move between fragmented habitats. By studying the movement patterns and behaviors of species like the jaguar in Central and South America, researchers can identify critical areas where corridors are needed. Understanding how animals use these corridors helps in designing them to be effective, ensuring that they provide safe passage and meet the ecological needs of the species.

Climate change poses one of the greatest threats to biodiversity, and behavioral research is key to understanding how species will adapt to changing conditions. Studying the behavioral responses of species to temperature changes, altered precipitation patterns, and shifting seasons helps predict their resilience and informs conservation strategies. For example, research on the timing of hibernation and migration in response to warming climates can guide conservation efforts to protect critical habitats and ensure that species have the resources they need to survive.

Behavioral research is fundamental to the success of reintroduction programs, where animals are released into areas where they have been extirpated. Understanding the behaviors necessary for survival in the wild, such as foraging, predator avoidance, and social interactions, is critical for the success of these programs. The reintroduction of wolves to Yellowstone National Park, for example, was informed by extensive behavioral studies that ensured the wolves would adapt to their new environment and reestablish their ecological role.

In conclusion, behavioral research is indispensable for effective conservation. It provides the insights needed to understand the complex interactions between species and their environments, informs the development of targeted conservation strategies, and helps mitigate human-wildlife conflicts. By studying animal behaviors, conservationists can create more effective and sustainable solutions, ensuring that wildlife populations thrive in the face of growing environmental challenges. The ongoing commitment to behavioral research will continue to be a cornerstone of conservation efforts, underpinning the protection and preservation of biodiversity for future generations.

Human-wildlife conflicts are an inevitable consequence of the expanding human footprint on the planet. As human populations grow and encroach upon natural habitats, encounters between people and wildlife become more frequent and often lead to negative outcomes for both. These conflicts can manifest in various ways, from crop raiding by elephants to livestock predation by wolves, and even to more subtle forms like competition for resources. Understanding the dynamics of these conflicts and developing effective resolutions is essential for both conservation efforts and human well-being.

In many rural communities, wildlife can pose a significant threat to livelihoods. Farmers, for example, often face challenges from animals like elephants, which can devastate entire fields of crops in a single night. This not only leads to economic losses but also fosters resentment towards the animals, sometimes resulting in retaliatory killings. To address such issues, it is crucial to develop strategies that protect both the livelihoods of local communities and the wildlife. One innovative solution has been the use of beehive fences. Elephants have a natural fear of bees, and placing beehives around fields has proven effective in deterring them. This method not only protects crops but also provides farmers with an additional source of income through honey production.

Livestock predation by large carnivores, such as lions and wolves, is another common source of conflict. These predators can inflict significant losses on herders, leading to retaliatory killings that threaten the survival of endangered species. To mitigate these conflicts, a combination of traditional knowledge and modern technology can be employed. Guardian animals, such as dogs, have been used for centuries to protect livestock. Modern advancements, like GPS tracking collars for herds and predators, can help monitor movements and prevent attacks. Additionally, compensation programs that reimburse farmers for livestock losses can reduce the financial burden and discourage retaliatory killings.

Urban areas are not immune to human-wildlife conflicts. As cities expand, they encroach on the habitats of various species, leading to encounters that can be dangerous for both humans and animals. Raccoons raiding garbage bins, coyotes preying on pets, and deer causing traffic accidents are common examples. Urban wildlife management requires a multifaceted approach that includes public education, habitat modification, and sometimes even relocation of problematic animals. Educating the public on how to coexist with wildlife, such as securing trash bins and avoiding feeding animals, can significantly reduce conflicts. Creating green corridors and wildlife crossings in urban planning can help animals safely navigate human-dominated landscapes.

One of the most challenging aspects of human-wildlife conflicts is the competition for natural resources. Freshwater sources, grazing lands, and forests are all vital for both human and wildlife populations. In regions where water is scarce, wildlife often competes with humans for access to this crucial resource. Constructing wildlife water points away from human settlements can help alleviate this competition. Similarly, managing grazing lands to ensure sustainable use by both livestock and wild herbivores can reduce conflicts. In forests, where logging and agriculture encroach on wildlife habitats, establishing community-managed conservation areas can provide a balance between human needs and wildlife conservation.-wildlife conflicts are not only a matter of immediate danger or economic loss; they also have cultural and psychological dimensions. In many cultures, wildlife holds significant symbolic and spiritual value. Elephants, tigers, and other iconic species are often revered and play important roles in local traditions and beliefs. When conflicts arise, they can lead to a loss of cultural heritage and identity. Conservationists must therefore work closely with local communities to develop conflict resolution strategies that respect and integrate cultural values. This involves engaging local leaders, incorporating traditional ecological knowledge, and ensuring that conservation initiatives provide tangible benefits to the community.

Preventing human-wildlife conflicts also requires addressing the underlying causes, which often stem from broader environmental and socio-economic issues. Habitat loss and fragmentation, driven by deforestation, agriculture, and urbanization, are primary drivers of conflict. Protecting and restoring habitats is therefore a fundamental aspect of conflict prevention. This can be achieved through the establishment of protected areas, reforestation projects, and sustainable land-use planning. Additionally, addressing socio-economic factors such as poverty and food insecurity can reduce the reliance on natural resources that often leads to conflict. Providing alternative livelihoods, promoting sustainable agriculture, and improving access to education and healthcare are all critical components of a holistic approach to conflict resolution.

In some cases, technological innovations offer promising solutions to human-wildlife conflicts. For example, the use of drones for monitoring wildlife movements can help prevent conflicts before they occur. In areas prone to crop raiding, drones equipped with thermal cameras can detect approaching animals and alert farmers in real-time, allowing them to take preventive measures. Similarly, advancements in fencing technology, such as solar-powered electric fences, provide effective barriers that can protect both livestock and crops. These technological solutions must be implemented in a way that is accessible and affordable to local communities to ensure their widespread adoption and effectiveness.

Collaboration and cooperation are essential for resolving human-wildlife conflicts. Conflicts often span large geographical areas and involve multiple stakeholders, including local communities, conservation organizations, government agencies, and sometimes even international bodies. Establishing platforms for dialogue and cooperation among these stakeholders is crucial for developing and implementing effective conflict resolution strategies. This involves sharing knowledge and resources, coordinating efforts, and ensuring that the voices and needs of local communities are heard and addressed.

Education and awareness are powerful tools in mitigating human-wildlife conflicts. By raising awareness about the importance of wildlife and the ecological roles they play, conservationists can foster a sense of stewardship and coexistence. Educational programs in schools, community workshops, and media campaigns can all contribute to changing attitudes and behaviors towards wildlife. Highlighting successful examples of conflict resolution and coexistence can inspire and motivate communities to adopt similar practices.

The role of policy and legislation cannot be overlooked in addressing human-wildlife conflicts. Effective laws and regulations that protect wildlife, manage natural resources, and support conflict resolution initiatives are essential. This includes enforcing anti-poaching laws, regulating land use, and providing legal frameworks for compensation and benefit-sharing programs. Policymakers must work closely with conservationists and local communities to ensure that policies are practical, enforceable, and aligned with the needs of all stakeholders.

Human-wildlife conflicts are complex and multifaceted, requiring a comprehensive and adaptive approach. By understanding the root causes, employing a variety of strategies, and fostering collaboration and education, we can develop effective solutions that protect both people and wildlife. The goal is not only to resolve conflicts but to create a harmonious coexistence where both humans and wildlife can thrive. This requires ongoing commitment, innovation, and a deep respect for the interconnectedness of all life on Earth.

Rehabilitating and Reintroducing Wildlife

Rehabilitating and reintroducing wildlife into their natural habitats is a delicate and complex process that requires a deep understanding of animal behavior, ecology, and the specific challenges faced by each species. This work is essential for conserving biodiversity, restoring ecosystems, and giving individual animals a second chance at life. The journey from rescue to release involves multiple stages, each with its own set of challenges and triumphs.

The first step in wildlife rehabilitation begins with the rescue. Animals may be injured, orphaned, or displaced due to human activities, natural disasters, or environmental changes. Each rescue operation is unique, requiring careful planning and swift action to ensure the safety and well-being of the animal. Rescuers must be trained to handle a variety of species, understanding their specific needs and stress responses. For example, a bird with a broken wing needs different care than a dehydrated tortoise or an orphaned bear cub. Initial assessments are critical to determine the extent of injuries and the appropriate course of treatment.

Once the animal is safely in a rehabilitation center, the focus shifts to medical care and recovery. Veterinarians play a pivotal role, using their expertise to diagnose and treat injuries or illnesses. This stage can be lengthy and requires patience and precision. For instance, a sea turtle suffering from ingested plastic debris may need surgery and a prolonged period of recovery. Similarly, an eagle with lead poisoning might undergo chelation therapy to remove toxins from its system. The goal is always to restore the animal to full health, but this is not always possible. In some cases, injuries are too severe, and the animal may need to be humanely euthanized to prevent further suffering.

Rehabilitation is not just about physical healing; it also involves preparing the animal for a return to the wild. This stage includes behavioral conditioning and environmental enrichment to ensure the animal can survive and thrive in its natural habitat. For example, predators like big cats or birds of prey need to hone their hunting skills, while herbivores must learn to forage effectively. Caregivers use various techniques to simulate natural conditions, such as hiding food to encourage foraging or using live prey to test hunting abilities. Social animals, like primates or elephants, require interaction with conspecifics to develop necessary social skills. This preparation is crucial for the animal's success post-release.

The actual reintroduction into the wild is a carefully orchestrated event, often involving multiple stakeholders, including conservationists, government agencies, and local communities. Selecting a suitable release site is paramount. This site must offer adequate food, water, shelter, and minimal human disturbance. Additionally, it should have a healthy existing population of the species or the capacity to support one. Detailed studies and surveys are conducted to identify the best locations. For example, the reintroduction of wolves into Yellowstone National Park was meticulously planned, considering the ecosystem's carrying capacity and the potential impacts on prey species and human activities.

Monitoring and support do not end with the release. Post-release monitoring is critical to assess the success of the reintroduction and to make necessary adjustments. This can involve tracking animals with GPS collars, observing their behavior, and ensuring they are integrating well into their new environment. For example, reintroduced lynxes might be tracked to see how they establish territories and interact with other predators. If an animal struggles to adapt, intervention may be necessary, which could include supplementary feeding or, in extreme cases, recapture and further rehabilitation.

Community involvement and education are integral to the success of wildlife reintroduction programs. Local communities often live in close proximity to release sites and can play a vital role in monitoring and protecting reintroduced species.

Educating the public about the importance of these efforts and how they can contribute helps build a supportive environment for the animals. In some cases, community members are trained as wildlife monitors, providing valuable data and fostering a sense of ownership and pride in conservation efforts. For instance, villagers near a reintroduction site for orangutans might be involved in patrols to prevent poaching and illegal logging.

Challenges in wildlife rehabilitation and reintroduction are numerous and varied. Disease transmission is a significant concern, as reintroduced animals can spread pathogens to wild populations or vice versa. Rigorous health screenings and quarantine protocols are essential to mitigate these risks. Additionally, human-wildlife conflicts can arise, particularly if animals venture into agricultural areas or human settlements. Strategies to mitigate these conflicts include creating buffer zones, using deterrents, and developing compensation schemes for affected communities.

Climate change adds another layer of complexity to rehabilitation and reintroduction efforts. Changing weather patterns, altered habitats, and shifting food availability can impact the success of reintroduced populations. Conservationists must consider these factors when planning releases, ensuring that the chosen sites have the resilience to support wildlife in a changing climate. Adaptive management practices, which involve continuously monitoring environmental conditions and adjusting strategies as needed, are crucial to address these dynamic challenges.

Success stories in wildlife rehabilitation and reintroduction are both inspiring and instructive. The return of the California condor from the brink of extinction is a testament to the effectiveness of coordinated conservation efforts. Captive breeding, rigorous health monitoring, and careful site selection have allowed these magnificent birds to soar again in the wild. Similarly, the reintroduction of the Arabian oryx in Oman, once extinct in the wild, showcases the power of international collaboration and long-term commitment to species recovery.

However, not all reintroduction efforts are successful, and failures provide valuable lessons. The reintroduction of the Pyrenean ibex, for example, faced setbacks due to genetic issues and habitat challenges. These experiences highlight the importance of thorough planning, genetic diversity, and the need for ongoing research and adaptation.

Rehabilitating and reintroducing wildlife is a labor of love and dedication, often requiring years of effort and collaboration across disciplines. It is a testament to human compassion and ingenuity, striving to correct the imbalances we have created and to restore the natural world. Each animal returned to the wild is a symbol of hope and a step towards a more harmonious coexistence with nature. As we look to the future, continued investment in these efforts is essential, ensuring that we not only preserve biodiversity but also enrich our own lives through the presence of wild, thriving ecosystems.

The Role of Zoos and Sanctuaries

Zoos and sanctuaries play a multifaceted role in wildlife conservation, education, and research. These institutions have evolved significantly over the years, shifting from mere attractions to crucial players in the global fight to preserve biodiversity. By providing safe havens for endangered species, fostering public awareness, and conducting critical research, zoos and sanctuaries contribute to the survival of many species that might otherwise face extinction.

Modern zoos are far removed from their predecessors, which were often criticized for inadequate care and small, barren enclosures. Today's zoos prioritize animal welfare, with expansive, enriched habitats designed to mimic natural environments as closely as possible. These spaces provide animals with the physical and mental stimulation they need to thrive. For example, large cat enclosures might include trees for climbing, open spaces for running, and hidden food to encourage natural hunting behaviors. Similarly, primate habitats often feature complex climbing structures, social groupings, and problem-solving activities to keep their agile minds engaged.

Zoos also play a vital role in breeding programs for endangered species. These programs, known as Species Survival Plans (SSPs), are meticulously managed to ensure genetic diversity and the overall health of captive populations. For instance, the SSP for the Amur leopard, one of the most endangered big cats in the world, coordinates breeding efforts across multiple zoos to maintain a genetically viable population. The ultimate goal of these programs is often to reintroduce individuals into the wild, bolstering dwindling populations and restoring ecological balance.

Sanctuaries, on the other hand, provide lifelong care for animals that cannot be released into the wild. These animals might be victims of illegal wildlife trade, former circus performers, or pets that owners can no longer care for. Sanctuaries offer a safe and nurturing environment where these animals can live out their lives with dignity. Unlike zoos, sanctuaries typically do not breed animals, focusing instead on providing the best possible care and enrichment for their residents. This care often includes specialized diets, medical treatment, and social opportunities to ensure the animals' well-being.

Education is another cornerstone of both zoos and sanctuaries. By connecting people with wildlife, these institutions foster a deeper appreciation for the natural world and the challenges it faces. Educational programs range from school visits and summer camps to interactive exhibits and keeper talks. For example, a zoo might offer behind-the-scenes tours where visitors can learn about the daily care of animals and the importance of conservation efforts. These experiences can inspire future generations of conservationists, scientists, and informed citizens who are committed to protecting the planet.

Research conducted in zoos and sanctuaries provides invaluable insights into animal behavior, physiology, and genetics. This research can inform conservation strategies, improve animal husbandry practices, and even contribute to medical advancements for both animals and humans. For instance, studies on elephant social structures and communication have shed light on their complex behaviors and needs, influencing both in-situ and ex-situ conservation efforts. Similarly, research on the reproductive biology of critically endangered species, such as the Sumatran rhinoceros, has been crucial in developing effective breeding programs.

Collaboration is key to the success of zoos and sanctuaries. These institutions often work together, as well as with universities, conservation organizations, and government agencies, to achieve their goals. For example, the Global Species Management Plan (GSMP) for the red panda involves zoos and sanctuaries worldwide, ensuring a coordinated approach to the species' conservation. This collaboration extends to sharing best practices, research findings, and even animals, to support breeding programs and enhance genetic diversity.

Despite their many contributions, zoos and sanctuaries face numerous challenges. One of the most significant is balancing the needs of individual animals with broader conservation goals. While breeding programs are essential for species survival, they must be managed carefully to avoid issues such as inbreeding or the spread of disease. Additionally, the decision to release animals into the wild is fraught with complexities, including ensuring the animals' survival and the impact on existing wild populations.

Funding is another critical challenge. Operating a zoo or sanctuary requires significant financial resources, from maintaining facilities and providing medical care to funding research and education programs. Many institutions rely on public support, grants, and donations to meet these needs. Economic downturns, changes in public interest, and competition for funding can all impact an institution's ability to carry out its mission effectively.

Public perception and ethical considerations also play a role in the operation of zoos and sanctuaries. Increasingly, there is a call for greater transparency and accountability in how these institutions care for their animals and contribute to conservation. This scrutiny can be a driving force for positive change, pushing zoos and sanctuaries to continually improve their practices and demonstrate their value to society.

In the face of these challenges, the future of zoos and sanctuaries looks promising, thanks to ongoing innovations and a growing commitment to conservation. Technological advancements, such as GPS tracking and genetic analysis, enhance research capabilities and improve animal welfare. Virtual reality and digital exhibits expand educational outreach, bringing the wonders of wildlife to a global audience. Moreover, a shift towards more naturalistic enclosures and enrichment practices reflects a deeper understanding of animal needs and behaviors.

Community engagement remains a crucial component of the mission of zoos and sanctuaries. By fostering connections between people and wildlife, these institutions help build a culture of conservation that extends beyond their gates. Volunteer programs, citizen science initiatives, and conservation partnerships all contribute to this effort, empowering individuals to take an active role in protecting the natural world.

In summary, zoos and sanctuaries serve as vital refuges for endangered species, centers for education and research, and beacons of hope in the fight to preserve biodiversity. Their work is complex and multifaceted, requiring a delicate balance of care, science, and public engagement. As we move forward, the continued evolution and improvement of these institutions will be essential in ensuring a future where both animals and humans can thrive. Through dedication, collaboration, and innovation, zoos and sanctuaries will remain at the forefront of conservation, inspiring and educating generations to come.